A Broader Perspective on Multiword Express 2007

Held in conjunction with ACL 2007

Prague, Czech Republic
28 June 2007

ISBN: 978-1-61738-520-9

Printed from e-media with permission by:

Curran Associates, Inc.
57 Morehouse Lane
Red Hook, NY 12571
www.proceedings.com

Some format issues inherent in the e-media version may also appear in this print version.

Printed by Curran Associates, Inc. (2010)

Association for Computational Linguistics
209 N. Eighth Street
Stroudsburg, Pennsylvania 18360

Phone: 1-570-476-8006
Fax: 1-570-476-0860

acl@aclweb.org

Preface

This volume contains the papers accepted for presentation at the workshop *A Broader Perspective on Multiword Expressions*. The workshop is endorsed by the Association for Computational Linguistics Special Interest Group on the Lexicon (SIGLEX) and is held in conjunction with the ACL 2007 Conference on June 28th, 2007 in Prague, Czech Republic.

In recent years, the NLP community has increasingly become aware of the problems that multiword expressions (MWEs) pose. A considerable amount of research has been conducted in this area, some within large research projects dedicated to MWEs. Although progress has been made especially in the area of multiword extraction, a number of fundamental questions remain unanswered. The goal of the workshop is to address some of these questions with oral and poster presentations, as well as general discussion period at the end of the workshop. In particular, we want to focus on the following topics:

- Is it sufficient to use purely statistical methods for the extraction of MWEs from corpora, or is it necessary to harness human knowledge and linguistic insights?
- To what extent can definitions and extraction procedures be generalised to other languages, other text types and other types of MWEs?
- What properties should be specified for MWEs or subtypes of MWEs in the lexicon? And can we detect these properties automatically with sufficient accuracy?
- What role do the semantics of MWEs play in NLP applications and can they be determined automatically from large corpora?

We received 23 submissions in total. Each submission was reviewed by at least two members of the program committee, who did not only give an overall verdict but also provided detailed comments to the authors. Due to the large number of interesting papers we had received and the fact that the workshop is only half-day, we decided on an unusual format including a poster session slot. This allowed us to accept ten papers for presentation at the workshop, four oral and six poster presentations. The poster session offers an opportunity to exhibit a wider range of approaches and points of view than would otherwise have been possible, and we hope it will thus initiate a lively and fruitful discussion period at the end of the workshop.

We would like to thank all the authors for submitting their research and the members of the program committee for their careful reviews and useful suggestions to the authors. We would also like to thank the ACL 2007 organising committee that made this workshop possible and SIGLEX for its endorsement.

Finally, we hope that this workshop will provide plentiful and tasty food for thought to all participants as well as readers of its proceedings.

Nicole Grégoire
Stefan Evert
Su Nam Kim

Organizers

Chairs:

Nicole Grégoire, University of Utrecht (The Netherlands)
Stefan Evert, University of Osnabrueck (Germany)
Su Nam Kim, University of Melbourne (Australia)

Program Committee:

Iñaki Alegria, University of the Basque Country (Spain)
Timothy Baldwin, Stanford University (USA); University of Melbourne (Australia)
Francis Bond, NTT Communication Science Laboratories (Japan)
Beatrice Daille, Nantes University (France)
Gael Dias, Beira Interior University (Portugal)
Kyo Kageura, University of Tokyo (Japan)
Anna Korhonen, University of Cambridge (UK)
Rosamund Moon, University of Birmingham (UK)
Diana McCarthy, University of Sussex (UK)
Eric Laporte, University of Marne-la-Vallee (France)
Preslav Nakov, University of California, Berkeley (USA)
Jan Odijk, University of Utrecht (The Netherlands)
Stephan Oepen, Stanford University (USA); University of Oslo (Norway)
Darren Pearce, University of Sussex (UK)
Scott Piao, University of Manchester (UK)
Violeta Seretan, University of Geneva (Switzerland)
Suzanne Stevenson, University of Toronto (Canada)
Beata Trawinski, University of Tuebingen (Germany)
Vivian Tsang, University of Toronto (Canada) Kiyoko Uchiyama, Keio University (Japan)
Ruben Urizar, University of the Basque Country (Spain)
Begoña Villada Moirón, University of Groningen (The Netherlands)
Aline Villavicencio, Federal University of Rio Grande do Sul (Brazil)

Table of Contents

Conference Program

Thursday, 28 June 2007

09:00–09:10 Opening remarks

09:10–10:50 Oral presentations

A Measure of Syntactic Flexibility for Automatically Identifying Multiword Expressions in Corpora
Colin Bannard

Distinguishing Subtypes of Multiword Expressions Using Linguistically-Motivated Statistical Measures
Afsaneh Fazly and Suzanne Stevenson

Design and Implementation of a Lexicon of Dutch Multiword Expressions
Nicole Grégoire

Semantics-based Multiword Expression Extraction
Tim Van de Cruys and Begoña Villada Moirón

10:50–11:20 Coffee break

11:20–11:40 Poster introduction (6x3 minutes)

11:40–12:30 Poster session

Spanish Adverbial Frozen Expressions
Dolors Català and Jorge Baptista

Pulling their Weight: Exploiting Syntactic Forms for the Automatic Identification of Idiomatic Expressions in Context
Paul Cook, Afsaneh Fazly and Suzanne Stevenson

Pauses as an Indicator of Psycholinguistically Valid Multi-Word Expressions (MWEs)?
Irina Dahlmann and Svenja Adolphs

Co-occurrence Contexts for Noun Compound Interpretation
Diarmuid Ó Séaghdha and Ann Copestake

Thursday, 28 June 2007 (continued)

A Measure of Syntactic Flexibility for Automatically Identifying Multiword Expressions in Corpora

Colin Bannard
Department of Developmental and Comparative Psychology
Max Planck Institute for Evolutionary Anthropology
Deutscher Platz 6
D-04103 Leipzig
colin.bannard@eva.mpg.de

Abstract

Natural languages contain many multi-word sequences that do not display the variety of syntactic processes we would expect given their phrase type, and consequently must be included in the lexicon as multiword units. This paper describes a method for identifying such items in corpora, focussing on English verb-noun combinations. In an evaluation using a set of dictionary-published MWEs we show that our method achieves greater accuracy than existing MWE extraction methods based on lexical association.

1 Introduction

A multi-word expression (henceforth MWE) is usually taken to be any word combination (adjacent or otherwise) that has some feature (syntactic, semantic or purely statistical) that cannot be predicted on the basis of its component words and/or the combinatorial processes of the language. Such units need to be included in any language description that hopes to account for actual usage. Lexicographers (for both printed dictionaries and NLP systems) therefore require well-motivated ways of automatically identifying units of interest. The work described in this paper is a contribution to this task.

Many linguists have offered classification schemes for MWEs. While these accounts vary in their terminology, they mostly focus on three different phenomena: collocation, non-compositionality and syntactic fixedness. In computational linguistics, a great deal of work has been done on the extraction of collocations in the last decade and a half (see Pecina (2005) for a survey). There have also been a number of papers focusing on the detection of semantic non-compositional items in recent years beginning with the work of Schone and Jurafsky (2001). The task of identifying syntactically-fixed phrases, however, has been much less explored. This third variety is the focus of the present paper. Languages contain many word combinations that do not allow the variation we would expect based solely on their grammatical form. In the most extreme case there are many phrases which seem to allow no syntactic variation whatsoever. These include phrases such as *by and large* and *in short*, which do not allow any morphological variation (**in shortest*) or internal modification (**by and pretty large*). We focus here on phrases that allow some syntactic variation, but do not allow other kinds.

The small amount of previous work on the identification of syntactic fixedness (Wermter and Hahn (2004), Fazly and Stevenson (2006)) has either focused on a single variation variety, or has only been evaluated for combinations of a small preselected list of words, presumably due to noise. In this paper we employ a syntactic parser, thus allowing us to include a wider range of syntactic features in our model. Furthermore we describe a statistical measure of variation that is robust enough to be freely evaluated over the full set of possible word combinations found in the corpus.

The remainder of our paper will be structured as follows. Section 2 will discuss the kinds of fixedness that we observe in our target phrase variety. Sec-

Proceedings of the Workshop on A Broader Perspective on Multiword Expressions, pages 1–8,
Prague, June 2007.

tion 3 will describe our model. Section 4 will evaluate the performance of the method and compare it to some other methods that have been described in the literature. Section 5 will describe some previous work on the problem, and section 6 will review our findings.

2 Syntactic Fixedness in English Verb Phrases

The experiments described here deal with one particular variety of phrase: English verb phrases of the form verb plus noun (e.g. *walk the dog*, *pull teeth*, *take a leaflet*). In a survey of the idiomatic phrases listed in the Collins Cobuild Dictionary of Idioms, Villavicencio and Copestake (2002) found this kind of idiom to account for more of the entries than any other. Riehemann (2001) performed a manual corpus analysis of verb and noun phrase idioms found in the Collins Cobuild Dictionary of Idioms. She found considerable fixedness with some phrases allowing no variation at all.

Based on this literature we identified three important kinds of non-morphological variation that such phrases can undergo, and which crucially have been observed to be restricted for particular combinations. These are as follows:

- Variation, addition or dropping of a determiner so that, for example, *run the show* becomes *run their show*, *make waves* becomes *make more waves*, or *strike a chord* becomes *strike chord* respectively.
- Modification of the noun phrase so that, for example, *break the ice* becomes *break the diplomatic ice*. We refer to this as internal modification.
- The verb phrase passivises so that, for example, *call the shots* is realised as *the shots were called by*.

3 Our Model

We use the written component of the BNC to make observations about the extent to which these variations are permitted by particular verb-noun combinations. In order to do this we need some way to a) identify such combinations, and b) identify when they are displaying a syntactic variation. In order to do both of these we utilise a syntactic parser.

We parse our corpus using the RASP system (Briscoe and Carroll, 2002). The system contains a LR probabilistic parser, based on a tag-sequence grammar. It is particularly suited to this task because unlike many contemporary parsers, it makes use of no significant information about the probability of seeing relationships between particular lexical items. Since we are looking here for cases where the syntactic behaviour of particular word combinations deviates from general grammatical patterns, it is desirable that the analysis we use has not already factored in lexical information. Example output can be seen in figure 1. We extract all verb and nouns pairs connected by an object relation in the parsed corpus. We are interested here in the object relationship between *buy* and *apartment*, and we can use the output to identify the variations that this phrase displays.

The first thing to note is that the phrase is passivised. *Apartment* is described as an object of *buy* by the "obj" relation that appears at the end of the line. Because of the passivisation, *apartment* is also described as a non-clausal subject of *buy* by the "ncmod" relation that appears at the beginning of the line. This presence of a semantic object that appears as a surface subject tells us that we are a dealing with a passive. The "ncmod" relation tells us that the adjective *largest* is a modifier of *apartment*. And finally, the "detmod" relation tells us that *the* is a determiner attached to *apartment*. We make a count over the whole corpus of the number of times each verb-object pair occurs, and the number of times it occurs with each relation of interest.

For passivisation and internal modification, a variation is simply the presence of a particular grammatical relation. The addition, dropping or variation of a determiner is not so straightforward. We are interested in the frequency with which each phrase varies from its dominant determiner status. We need therefore to determine what this dominant status is for each item. A verb and noun object pair where the noun has no determiner relation is recorded as having no determiner. This is one potential determiner status. The other varieties of status are defined by the kind of determiner that is appended. The RASP parser uses the very rich CLAWS-2 tagset. We con-

```
(|ncsubj| |buy+ed:6_VVN| |apartment:3_NN1| |obj|)
(|arg_mod| |by:7_II| |buy+ed:6_VVN| |couple:10_NN1| |subj|)
(|ncmod| _ |apartment:3_NN1| |largest:2_JJT|)
(|detmod| _ |apartment:3_NN1| |The:1_AT|)
(|ncmod| _ |couple:10_NN1| |Swedish:9_JJ|)
(|detmod| _ |couple:10_NN1| |a:8_AT1|)
(|mod| _ |buy+ed:6_VVN| |immediately:5_RR|)
(|aux| _ |buy+ed:6_VVN| |be+ed:4_VBDZ|)
```

Figure 1: RASP parse of sentence *The largest apartment was immediately bought by a Swedish couple.*

sider each of these tags as a different determiner status. Once the determiner status of all occurrences has been recorded, the dominant status for each item is taken to be the status that occurs most frequently. The number of variations is taken to be the number of times that the phrase occurs with any other status.

3.1 Quantifying variation

We are interested here in measuring the degree of syntactic variation allowed by each verb-object pair found in our corpus. Firstly we use the counts that we extracted above to estimate the probability of each variation for each combination, employing a Laplace estimator to deal with zero counts.

A straightforward product of these probabilities would give us the probability of free variation for a given verb-object pair. We need, however, to consider the fact that each phrase has a prior probability of variation derived from the probability of variation of the component words. Take passivisation for example. Some verbs are more prone to passivisation than others. The degree of passivisation of a phrase will therefore depend to a large extent upon the passivisation habits of the component verb.

What we want is an estimate of the extent to which the probability of variation for that combination deviates from the variation we would expect based on the variation we observe for its component words. For this we use conditional pointwise mutual information. Each kind of variation is associated with a single component word. Passivisation is associated with the verb. Internal modification and determiner variation are associated with the object. We calculate the mutual information of the syntactic variation x and the word y given the word z, as seen in equation 1. In the case of passivisation z will be the verb and y will be the object. In the case of internal modification and determiner variation z will be the object.

$$\begin{aligned} I(x;y|z) &= H(x|z) - H(x|y,z) \\ &= -\,log_2\, p(x|z) - [-\log_2\, p(x|y,z)] \\ &= -\,log_2\, p(x|z) + \log_2\, p(x|y,z) \\ &= log_2 \frac{p(x|y,z)}{p(x|z)} \end{aligned} \quad (1)$$

Conditional pointwise mutual information tells us the amount of information in bits that y provides about x (and vice versa) given z (see e.g. MacKay (2003)). If a variation occurs for a given word pair with greater likelihood than we would expect based on the frequency of seeing that same variation with the relevant component word, then the mutual information will be high. We want to find the information that is gained about all the syntactic variations by a particular verb and object combination. We therefore calculate the information gained about all the verb-relevant syntactic variations (passivisation) by the addition of the object, and the information gained about all the object relevant variations (internal modification and determiner dropping, variation or addition) by the addition of the verb. Summing these, as in equation 2 then gives us the total information gained about syntactic variation for the word pair W, and we take this as our measure of the degree of syntactic flexibility for this pair.

$$\begin{aligned} SynVar(W) = &\sum_i^n I(VerbVar_i; Obj|Verb) \\ &+ \sum_j^n I(ObjVar_j; Verb|Obj) \end{aligned} \quad (2)$$

4 Evaluation

This paper aims to provide a method for highlighting those verb plus noun phrases that are syntactically fixed and consequently need to be included in the lexicon. This is intended as a tool for lexicographers. We hypothesize that in a list that has been inversely ranked with the variability measure valid MWEs will occur at the top.

The evaluation procedure used here (first suggested by Evert and Krenn (2001) for evaluating measures of lexical association) involves producing and evaluating just such a ranking. The RASP parser identifies 979,156 unique verb-noun pairs in the BNC. The measure of syntactic flexibility was used to inverse rank these items (the most fixed first).[1] This ranking was then evaluated using a list of idioms taken from published dictionaries, by observing how many of the gold standard items were found in each top n, and calculating the accuracy score. [2] By reason of the diverse nature of MWEs, these lists can be expected to contain many MWEs that are not syntactically fixed, giving us a very low upper bound. However this seems to us the evaluation that best reflects the application for which the measure is designed. The list of gold standard idioms we used were taken from the Longman Dictionary of English idioms (Long and Summers, 1979) and the SAID Syntactically Annotated Idiom Dataset (Kuiper et al., 2003). Combining the two dictionaries gave us a list of 1109 unique verb-noun pairs, 914 of which were identified in the BNC.

In order to evaluate the performance of our technique it will be useful to compare its results with the ranks of scores that can be obtained by other means. A simple method of sorting items available to the corpus lexicographer that might expected to give reasonable performance is item frequency. We take this as our baseline. In the introduction we referred to multiple varieties of MWE. One such variety is the collocation. Although the collocation is a different variety of MWE, any dictionary will contain collocations as well as syntactically fixed phrases. The collocation has received more attention than any other variety of MWE and it will therefore be useful to compare our measure with these methods as state-of-the-art extraction techniques. We report the performance obtained when we rank our candidate items using all four collocation extraction techniques described in Manning and Schutze (1999) : t-score, mutual information, log likelihood and χ^2.

4.1 Results

Figure 2 provides a plot of the accuracy score each sample obtains when evaluated using the superset of the two dictionaries for all samples from n = 1 to n = 5,000.

Included in figure 2 are the scores obtained when we inverse ranked using the variation score for each individual feature, calculated with equation 1. There is notable divergence in the performance of the different features. The best performing feature is passivisation, followed by internal modification. Determiner variation performs notably worse for all values of n.

We next wanted to look at combinations of these features using equation 2. We saw that the various syntactic variations achieved very different scores when used in isolation, and it was by no means certain that combining all features would the best approach. Nonetheless we found that the best scores were achieved by combining all three - an accuracy of 18%, 14.2 and 5.86% for n of 100, 1000 and 5000 respectively. This can be see in figure 2. The results achieved with frequency ranking can also be seen in the plot.

The accuracy achieved by the four collocation measures can be seen plotted in figure 3. The best performers are the t-score and the log-likelihood ratio, with MI and χ-squared performing much worse. The best score for low values of n is t-score, with log-likelihood overtaking for larger values. The best performing collocation measures often give a performance that is only equal to and often worse than raw frequency. This is consistent with results reported by Evert and Krenn (2001). Our best syntactic variation method outperforms all the collocation extraction techniques.

We can see, then, that our method is outperforming frequency ranking and the various collocation measures in terms of accuracy. A major claim we

[1] Any ties were dealt with by generating a random number for each item and ranking the drawn items using this.

[2] Note that because the number of candidate items in each sample is fixed, the relative performance of any two methods will be the same for recall as it is for precision. In such circumstances the term accuracy is preferred.

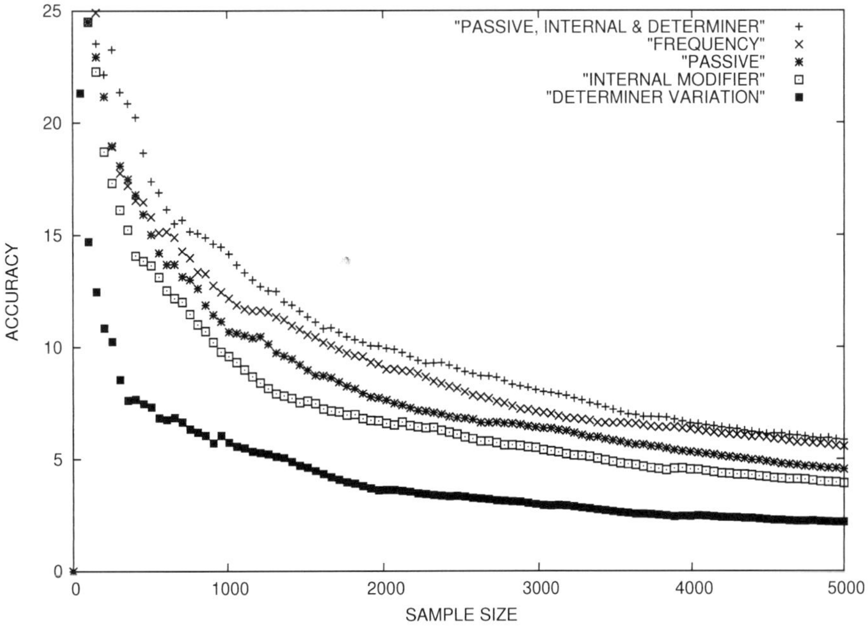

Figure 2: Accuracy by sample size for syntactic variation measures

are making for the method however is that it extracts a different kind of phrase. A close examination tells us that this is the case. Table 1 lists the top 25 verb-noun combinations extracted using our best performing combination of features, and those extracted using frequency ranking. As can be see there is no overlap between these lists. In the top 50 items there is an overlap of 3 between the two lists. Over the top 100 items of the two lists there is only an overlap of 6 items and over the top 1000 there is an overlap of only 98.

This small overlap compares favourably with that found for the collocation scores. While they produce ranks that are different from pure frequency, the collocation measures are still based on relative frequencies. The two high-performing collocation measures, t-score and log-likelihood have overlap with frequency of 795 and 624 out of 1000 respectively. This tells us that the collocation measures are significantly duplicating the information available from frequency ranking. The item overlap between t-score items and those extracted using the the best-performing syntactic variation measure is 116. The overlap between syntactic variation and log-likelihood items is 108. This small overlap tells us that our measure is extracting very different items from the collocation measures.

Given that our measure appears to be pinpointing a different selection of items from those highlighted by frequency ranking or lexical association, we next want looked at combining the two sources of information. We test this by ranking our candidate list using frequency and using the most consistently well-performing syntactic variation measure in two separate runs, and then adding together the two ranks achieved using the two methods for each item. The items are then reranked using the resulting sums. When this ranking is evaluated against the dictionaries it gives the scores plotted in figure 3 - a clearly better performance than syntactic fixedness or frequency alone for samples of 1000 and above.

Having reported all scores we now want to measure whether any of them are beating frequency ranking at a level that is statistically significant.

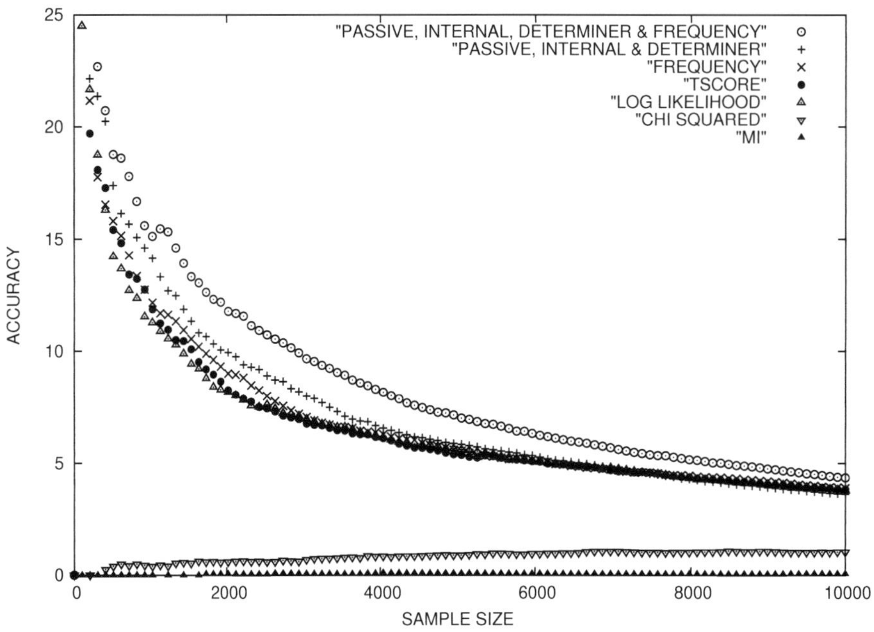

Figure 3: Accuracy by sample size for lexical association measures

In order to do this we pick three values of n (100,1000 and 5000) and examine whether the accuracy achieved by our method are greater than those achieved with frequency ranking at a level that is significantly greater than chance. Conventional significance testing is problematic for this task. Rather than using a significance test that relies upon an assumed distribution, then, we will use a computationally-intensive randomization test of significance called stratified shuffling. This technique works by estimating the difference that might occur between scores by chance through a simulation (see (Cohen, 1995) for details). As is standard we perform 10,000 shuffle iterations.

The results for our three chosen values of n can be seen in table 2. We accept any result of $p < 0.05$ as significant, and scores that achieve this level of significance are shown in bold. As an additional check on performance we also extend our evaluation. In any evaluation against a gold standard resource, there is a risk that the performance of a technique is particular to the lexical resource used and will not generalise. For this reason we will here report results achieved using not only the combined set but also each dictionary in isolation. If the technique is effective then we would expect it to perform well for both resources.

We can see that our syntactic variation measures perform equal to or better than frequency over both dictionaries in isolation for samples of 1000 and 5000. The good performance against two data sets tells us that the performance does generalise beyond a single resource. For the Longman dictionary, the accuracy achieved by the syntactic variation measure employing the three best performing features ("P, I and D") is significantly higher (at a level of $p < 0.05$) than that achieved when ranking with frequency for sample sizes of 1000 and 5000. The ranking achieved using the combination of syntactic fixedness and frequency information produces a result that is significant over all items for samples of 1000 and 5000. By contrast, none of the collocation scores perform significantly better than frequency. [3]

[3] As very low frequency items have been observed to cause

		Syntactic Variation		Collocation			
DICTIONARY	Freq	P,I &D	P,I,D &Freq	t	MI	LLR	χ^2
Top 100 items							
LONGMANS	14	21	15	16	0	13	0
SAID	21	17	17	23	0	17	0
BOTH	28	18	25	32	0	25	0
Top 1000 items							
LONGMANS	6.6	**10.4**	**10.2**	6.3	0	6.5	0.3
SAID	9.1	9	9.9	9	0	8.1	0.2
BOTH	12.2	14.2	**15.2**	12	0	11.4	0.4
Top 5000 items							
LONGMANS	3.24	**4.28**	**4.84**	3.12	0.06	3.44	0.58
SAID	3.86	3.56	**4.54**	3.68	0.04	3.86	0.54
BOTH	5.56	5.86	**7.68**	5.34	0.04	5.66	0.88

Table 2: Accuracy for top 100, 1000 and 5000 items (scores beating frequency at $p < 0.05$ are in bold)

An important issue for future research is how much the performance of our measure is affected by the technology used. In an evalutaion of RASP, Preiss (2003) reports an precision of 85.83 and recall of 78.48 for the direct object relation, 69.45/57.72 for the "ncmod" relation, and 91.15/98.77 for the "detmod" relation. There is clearly some variance here, but it is not easy to see any straightforward relationship with our results. The highest performance relation ("detmod") was our least informative feature. Meanwhile our other two features both rely on the "ncmod" relation. One way to address this issue in future research will be to replicate using multiple parsers.

5 Previous work

Wermter and Hahn (2004) explore one kind of syntactic fixedness: the (non-)modifiability of preposition-noun-verb combinations in German. They extract all preposition-noun-verb combinations from a corpus of German news text, and identify all the supplementary lexical information that occurs between the preposition and the verb. For each phrase they calculate the probability of seeing each piece of supplementary material, and take this as its degree of fixedness. A final score is then calculated by taking the product of this score and the probability of occurrence of the phrase. They then manually evaluated how many true MWEs occurred in the top n items at various values of n. Like us they report that their measure outperformed t-score, log likelihood ratio and frequency.

Fazly and Stevenson (2006) propose a measure for detecting the syntactic fixedness of English verb phrases of the same variety as us. They use a set of regular patterns to identify, for particular word combinations (including one of a chosen set of 28 frequent "basic" verbs), the probability of occurrence in passive voice, with particular determiners and in plural form. They then calculate the relative entropy of this probability distribution for the particular word pair and the probabilities observed over all the word combinations. As we pointed out in section 3.1 a comparison with all verbs is problematic as each verb will have its own probability of variation, and this perhaps explains their focus on a small set of verbs. They use a development set to establish a threshold on what constitutes relative fixedness and calculate the accuracy. This threshhold gives over the set of 200 items, half of which were found in a dictionary and hence considered MWEs and half weren't. They report an accuracy of 70%, against a 50% baseline. While this is promising, their use of a small selection of items of a particular kind in their evaluation makes it somewhat difficult to assess.

problems for collocation measures, we experimented with various cutoffs up to an occurence rate of 5. We found that this did not lead to any significant difference from frequency.

	FREQUENCY	P,I & D
1	take place	follow suit
2	have effect	draw level
3	shake head	give rise
4	have time	part company
5	take part	see chapter
6	do thing	give moment
7	make decision	open fire
8	have idea	run counter
9	play role	take refuge
10	play part	clear throat
11	open door	speak volume
12	do job	please contact
13	do work	leave net
14	make sense	give way
15	have chance	see page
16	make use	catch sight
17	ask question	cite argument
18	spend time	see table
19	take care	check watch
20	have problem	list engagement
21	take step	go bust
22	take time	change subject
23	take action	change hand
24	find way	keep pace
25	have power	see paragraph

Table 1: Top 25 phrases

6 Discussion

Any lexicon must contain multiword units as well as individual words. The linguistic literature contains claims for the inclusion of multiword items in the lexicon on the basis of a number of linguistic dimensions. One of these is syntactic fixedness. This paper has shown that by quantifying the syntactic fixedness of verb-noun phrases we can identify a gold standard set of dictionary MWEs with a greater accuracy than the lexical association measures that have hitherto dominated the literature, and that, perhaps more crucially, we can identify a different set of expressions, not available using existing techniques.

Acknowledgements

Thanks to Tim Baldwin, Francis Bond, Ted Briscoe, Chris Callison-Burch, Mirella Lapata, Alex Lascarides, Andrew Smith, Takaaki Tanaka and two anonymous reviewers for helpful ideas and comments.

References

Ted Briscoe and John Carroll. 2002. Robust accurate statistical annotation of general text. In *Proceedings of LREC-2003.*

P. Cohen. 1995. *Empirical Methods for Artificial Intelligence.* MIT Press.

Stefan Evert and Brigitte Krenn. 2001. Methods for the qualitative evaluation of lexical association measures. In *Proceedings of ACL-2001.*

Afsaneh Fazly and Suzanne Stevenson. 2006. Automatically constructing a lexicon of verb phrase idiomatic combinations. In *Proceedings of EACL-2006.*

Koenraad Kuiper, Heather McCann, and Heidi Quinn. 2003. A syntactically annotated idiom database (said), v,1.

Thomas H. Long and Della Summers. 1979. *Longman Dictionary of English Idioms.* Longman Dictionaries.

David J.C. MacKay. 2003. *Information Theory, Inference and Learning Algorithms.* Cambridge University Press.

C. Manning and H. Schutze. 1999. *Foundations of Statistical Natural Language Processing.* MIT Press, Cambridge, USA.

Pavel Pecina. 2005. An extensive empirical study of collocation extraction methods. In *Proceedings of the ACL-2005 Student Research Workshop.*

Judita Preiss. 2003. Using grammatical relations to compare parsers. In *Proceedings of EACL-03.*

Suzanne Riehemann. 2001. *A Constructional Approach to Idioms and Word Formation.* Ph.D. thesis, Stanford University.

Patrick Schone and Dan Jurafsky. 2001. Is knowledge-free induction of multiword unit dictionary headwords a solved problem? In *Proceedings of EMNLP-2001.*

Aline Villavicencio and Ann Copestake. 2002. On the nature of idioms. *LinGO Working Paper No. 2002-04.*

Joachim Wermter and Udo Hahn. 2004. Collocation extraction based on modifiability statistics. In *Proceedings of COLING-2004.*

Distinguishing Subtypes of Multiword Expressions Using Linguistically-Motivated Statistical Measures

Afsaneh Fazly
Department of Computer Science
University of Toronto
Toronto, Canada
afsaneh@cs.toronto.edu

Suzanne Stevenson
Department of Computer Science
University of Toronto
Toronto, Canada
suzanne@cs.toronto.edu

Abstract

We identify several classes of multiword expressions that each require a different encoding in a (computational) lexicon, as well as a different treatment within a computational system. We examine linguistic properties pertaining to the degree of semantic idiosyncrasy of these classes of expressions. Accordingly, we propose statistical measures to quantify each property, and use the measures to automatically distinguish the classes.

1 Motivation

Multiword expressions (MWEs) are widely used in written language as well as in colloquial speech. An MWE is composed of two or more words that together form a single unit of meaning, e.g., *frying pan*, *take a stroll*, and *kick the bucket*. Most MWEs behave like any phrase composed of multiple words, e.g., their components may be separated, as in *She took a relaxing stroll along the beach*. Nonetheless, MWEs are distinct from multiword phrases because they involve some degree of semantic idiosyncrasy, i.e., the overall meaning of an MWE diverges from the combined contribution of its constituent parts. Because of their frequency and their peculiar behaviour, MWEs pose a great challenge to the creation of natural language processing (NLP) systems (Sag et al., 2002). NLP applications, such as semantic parsing and machine translation should not only identify MWEs, but also should know how to treat them when they are encountered.

Semantic idiosyncrasy is a matter of degree (Nunberg et al., 1994). The idiom *shoot the breeze* is largely idiosyncratic, because its meaning ("to chat") does not have much to do with the meaning of *shoot* or *breeze*. MWEs such as *give a try* ("try") and *make a decision* ("decide") are semantically less idiosyncratic (more predictable). These are MWEs because the overall meaning of the expression diverges from the combined meanings of the constituents. Nonetheless, there is some degree of predictability in their meanings that makes them distinct from idioms. In these, the complement of the verb (here, a noun) determines the primary meaning of the overall expression. This class of expressions is referred to as light verb constructions (LVCs) in the linguistics literature (Miyamoto, 2000; Butt, 2003).

Clearly, a computational system should distinguish idioms and LVCs, both from each other, and from similar-on-the-surface (literal) phrases such as *shoot the bird* and *give a present*. Idioms are largely idiosyncratic; a computational lexicographer thus may decide to list idioms such as *shoot the breeze* in a lexicon along with their idiomatic meanings. In contrast, the meaning of MWEs such as *make a decision* can be largely predicted, given that they are LVCs. Table 1 shows the different underlying semantic structure of a sentence containing an idiom (*shoot the breeze*) and a sentence containing an LVC (*give a try*). As can be seen, such MWEs should also be treated differently when translated into another language. Note that in contrast to a literal combination, such as *shoot the bird*, for idioms and LVCs, the number of arguments expressed syntactically may differ from the number of the semantic participants.

Many NLP applications also need to distinguish another group of MWEs that are less idiosyncratic

Proceedings of the Workshop on A Broader Perspective on Multiword Expressions, pages 9–16,
Prague, June 2007. ©2007 Association for Computational Linguistics

Class	English sentence	Semantic representation	French translation
Literal	*Jill and Tim shot the bird.*	(event/SHOOT :agent ("*Jill* ∧ *Tim*") :theme ("*bird*"))	*Jill et Tim ont abattu l'oiseau.* *Jill and Tim shot down the bird.*
Abstract	*Jill makes a living singing in pubs.*	(event/EARN-MONEY :agent ("*Jill*"))	*Jill gagne sa vie en chantant dans des bars.* *Jill makes a living by singing in the pubs.*
LVC	*Jill gave the lasagna a try.*	(event/TRY :agent ("*Jill*") :theme ("*lasagna*"))	*Jill a essayé le lasagne.* *Jill tried the lasagna.*
Idiom	*Jill and Tim shot the breeze.*	(event/CHAT :agent ("*Jill* ∧ *Tim*"))	*Jill et Tim ont bavardé.* *Jill and Tim chatted.*

Table 1: Sample English MWEs and their translation in French.

than idioms and LVCs, but more so than literal combinations. Examples include *give confidence* and *make a living*. These are idiosyncratic because the meaning of the verb is a metaphorical (abstract) extension of its basic physical semantics. Moreover, they often take on certain connotations beyond the compositional combination of their constituent meanings. They thus exhibit behaviour often attributed to collocations, e.g., they appear with greater frequency than semantically similar combinations. For example, searching on Google, we found much higher frequency for *give confidence* compared to *grant confidence*. As can be seen in Table 1, an abstract combination such as *make a living*, although largely compositional, may not translate word-for-word. Rather, it should be translated taking into account that the verb has a metaphorical meaning, different from its basic semantics.

Here, we focus on a particular class of English MWEs that are formed from the combination of a verb with a noun in its direct object position, referred to as verb+noun combinations. Specifically, we provide a framework for identifying members of the following semantic classes of verb+noun combinations: (i) literal phrases (LIT), (ii) abstract combinations (ABS), (iii) light verb constructions (LVC), and (iv) idiomatic combinations (IDM). Section 2 elaborates on the linguistic properties related to the differences in the degree of semantic idiosyncrasy observed in members of the above four classes. In Section 3, we propose statistical measures for quantifying each of these properties, and use them as features for type classification of verb+noun combinations. Section 4 and Section 5 present an evaluation of our proposed measures. Section 6 discusses the related studies, and Section 7 concludes the paper.

2 Semantic Idiosyncrasy: Linguistic Properties

Linguists and lexicographers often attribute certain characteristics to semantically idiosyncratic expressions. Some of the widely-known properties are institutionalization, lexicosyntactic fixedness, and non-compositionality (Cowie, 1981; Gibbs and Nayak, 1989; Moon, 1998). The following paragraphs elaborate on each property, as well as on its relevance to the identification of the classes under study.

Institutionalization is the process through which a combination of words becomes recognized and accepted as a semantic unit involving some degree of semantic idiosyncrasy. IDMs, LVCs, and ABS combinations are institutionalized to some extent.

Lexicosyntactic fixedness refers to some degree of lexical and syntactic restrictiveness in a semantically idiosyncratic expression. An expression is lexically fixed if the substitution of a semantically similar word for any of its constituents does not preserve its original meaning (e.g., compare *spill the beans* and *spread the beans*). In contrast to LIT and ABS combinations, IDMs and LVCs are expected to exhibit lexical fixedness to some extent.

An expression is syntactically fixed if it cannot undergo syntactic variations and at the same time retain its original semantic interpretation. IDMs and LVCs are known to show strong preferences for the syntactic patterns they appear in (Cacciari and Tabossi, 1993; Brinton and Akimoto, 1999). E.g., compare

Joe gave a groan with ?*A groan was given by Joe*, and *Tim kicked the bucket* with **Tim kicked the buckets* (in the idiom reading). Nonetheless, the type and degree of syntactic fixedness in LVCs and IDMs are different. For example, most LVCs prefer the pattern in which the noun is introduced by the indefinite article *a* (as in *give a try* and *make a decision*), whereas this is not the case with IDMs (e.g., *shoot the breeze* and *kick the bucket*). IDMs and LVCs may also exhibit preferences with respect to adjectival modification of their noun constituent. LVCs are expected to appear both with and without an adjectival modifier, as in *give a (loud) groan* and *make a (wise) decision*. IDMs, on the other hand, mostly appear either with an adjective, as in *keep an open mind* (cf. ?*keep a mind*), or without, as in *shoot the breeze* (cf. ?*shoot the fun breeze*).

Non-compositionality refers to the situation where the meaning of a word combination deviates from the meaning emerging from a word-by-word interpretation of it. IDMs are largely non-compositional, whereas LVCs are semi-compositional since their meaning can be mainly predicted from the noun constituent. ABS and LIT combinations are expected to be largely compositional.

None of the above-mentioned properties are sufficient criteria by themselves for determining which semantic class a given verb+noun combination belongs to. Moreover, semantic properties of the constituents of a combination are also known to be relevant for determining its class (Uchiyama et al., 2005). Verbs may exhibit strong preferences for appearing in MWEs from a particular class, e.g., *give*, *take* and *make* commonly form LVCs. The semantic category of the noun is also relevant to the type of MWE, e.g., the noun constituent of an LVC is often a predicative one. We hypothesize that if we look at evidence from all these different sources, we will find members of the same class to be reasonably similar, and members of different classes to be notably different.

3 Statistical Measures of Semantic Idiosyncrasy

This section introduces measures for quantifying the properties of idiosyncratic MWEs, mentioned in the previous section. The measures will be used as features in a classification task (see Sections 4–5).

3.1 Measuring Institutionalization

Corpus-based approaches often assess the degree of institutionalization of an expression by the frequency with which it occurs. Raw frequencies drawn from a corpus are not reliable on their own, hence association measures such as pointwise mutual information (PMI) are also used in many NLP applications (Church et al., 1991). PMI of a verb+noun combination $\prec v, n \succ$ is defined as:

$$\begin{aligned} \text{PMI}\,(v,\,n) &\doteq \log \frac{P(v,\,n)}{P(v)\,P(n)} \\ &\approx \log \frac{f(*,\,*)f(v,\,n)}{f(v,*)\,f(*,\,n)} \end{aligned} \qquad (1)$$

where all frequency counts are calculated over verb–object pairs in a corpus. We use both frequency and PMI of a verb+noun combination to measure its degree of institutionalization. We refer to this group of measures as `INST`.

3.2 Measuring Fixedness

To measure fixedness, we use statistical measures of lexical, syntactic, and overall fixedness that we have developed in a previous study (Fazly and Stevenson, 2006), as well as some new measures we introduce here. The following paragraphs give a brief description of each.

$\text{Fixedness}_{\text{lex}}$ quantifies the degree of lexical fixedness of the target combination, $\prec v, n \succ$, by comparing its strength of association (measured by PMI) with those of its lexical variants. Like Lin (1999), we generate lexical variants of the target automatically by replacing either the verb or the noun constituent by a semantically similar word from the automatically-built thesaurus of Lin (1998). We then use a standard statistic, the z-score, to calculate $\text{Fixedness}_{\text{lex}}$:

$$\text{Fixedness}_{\text{lex}}(v,\,n) \doteq \frac{\text{PMI}(v,\,n) - \overline{\text{PMI}}}{std} \qquad (2)$$

where $\overline{\text{PMI}}$ is the mean and std the standard deviation over the PMI of the target and all its variants.

$\text{Fixedness}_{\text{syn}}$ quantifies the degree of syntactic fixedness of the target combination, by comparing its behaviour in text with the behaviour of a typical verb–object, both defined as probability distributions over a predefined set of patterns. We use a standard information-theoretic measure, relative entropy,

v	det:NULL	n_{sg}	v	det:NULL	n_{pl}
v	det:*a/an*	n_{sg}			
v	det:*the*	n_{sg}	v	det:*the*	n_{pl}
v	det:DEM	n_{sg}	v	det:DEM	n_{pl}
v	det:POSS	n_{sg}	v	det:POSS	n_{pl}
v	det:OTHER	$n_{sg,pl}$	det:ANY $n_{sg,pl}$ be $v_{passive}$		

Table 2: Patterns for syntactic fixedness measure.

to calculate the divergence between the two distributions as follows:

$$\begin{aligned} &\text{Fixedness}_{\text{syn}}\,(v,\,n) \\ &\doteq\; D(P(pt|v,n)\,||\,P(pt)) \\ &=\; \sum_{pt_k \in \mathcal{P}} P(pt_k|\,v,\,n)\log\frac{P(pt_k|\,v,\,n)}{P(pt_k)} \end{aligned} \quad (3)$$

where $\mathcal{P}$ is the set of patterns (shown in Table 2) known to be relevant to syntactic fixedness in LVCs and IDMs. $P(pt|\,v,\,n)$ represents the syntactic behaviour of the target, and $P(pt)$ represents the typical syntactic behaviour over all verb–object pairs.

$\text{Fixedness}_{\text{syn}}$ does not show which syntactic pattern the target prefers the most. We thus use an additional measure, $\text{Pattern}_{\text{dom}}$, to determine the dominant pattern for the target:

$$\text{Pattern}_{\text{dom}}(v,\,n) \;\doteq\; \underset{pt_k \in \mathcal{P}}{\text{argmax}}\, f(v,\,n,\,pt_k) \quad (4)$$

In addition to the individual measures of fixedness, we use $\text{Fixedness}_{\text{overall}}$, which quantifies the degree of overall fixedness of the target:

$$\begin{aligned} &\text{Fixedness}_{\text{overall}}\,(v,\,n) \\ &\doteq\; \alpha\;\text{Fixedness}_{\text{syn}}\,(v,\,n) \\ &\quad +(1-\alpha)\;\text{Fixedness}_{\text{lex}}\,(v,\,n) \end{aligned} \quad (5)$$

where α weights the relative contribution of lexical and syntactic fixedness in predicting semantic idiosyncrasy.

$\text{Fixedness}_{\text{adj}}$ quantifies the degree of fixedness of the target combination with respect to adjectival modification of the noun constituent. It is similar to the syntactic fixedness measure, except here there are only two patterns that mark the presence or absence of an adjectival modifier preceding the noun:

$$\text{Fixedness}_{\text{adj}}(v,\,n) \;\doteq\; D(P(a_i|v,n)\,||\,P(a_i)) \quad (6)$$

where $a_i \in \{\text{present}, \text{absent}\}$. $\text{Fixedness}_{\text{adj}}$ does not determine which pattern of modification the target combination prefers most. We thus add another measure—the odds of modification—to capture this:

$$\text{Odds}_{\text{adj}}(v,\,n) \;\doteq\; \frac{P(a_i = \text{present}|v,n)}{P(a_i = \text{absent}|v,n)} \quad (7)$$

Overall, we use six measures related to fixedness; we refer to the group as FIXD.

3.3 Measuring Compositionality

Compositionality of an expression is often approximated by comparing the "context" of the expression with the contexts of its constituents. We measure the degree of compositionality of a target verb+noun combination, $t = \prec v, n\succ$, in a similar fashion.

We take the context of the target (t) and each of its constituents (v and n) to be a vector of the frequency of nouns cooccurring with it within a window of ± 5 words. We then measure the "similarity" between the target and each of its constituents, $\text{Sim}_{\text{dist}}\,(t,\,v)$ and $\text{Sim}_{\text{dist}}\,(t,\,n)$, using the cosine measure.[1]

Recall that an LVC can be roughly paraphrased by a verb that is morphologically related to its noun constituent, e.g., *to make a decision* nearly means *to decide*. For each target t, we thus add a third measure, $\text{Sim}_{\text{dist}}\,(t,\,rv)$, where rv is a verb morphologically related to the noun constituent of t, and is automatically extracted from WordNet (Fellbaum, 1998).[2]

We use abbreviation COMP to refer to the group of measures related to compositionality.

3.4 The Constituents

Recall that semantic properties of the constituents of a verb+noun combination are expected to be relevant to its semantic class. We thus add two simple feature groups: (i) the verb itself (VERB); and (ii) the semantic category of the noun according to WordNet (NSEM). We take the semantic category of a noun to be the ancestor of its first sense in the hypernym hierarchy of WordNet 2.1, cut at the level of the children

[1]Our preliminary experiments on development data from Fazly and Stevenson (2006) revealed that the cosine measure and a window size of ± 5 words resulted in the best performance.

[2]If no such verb exists, $\text{Sim}_{\text{dist}}\,(t,\,rv)$ is set to zero. If more than one verb exist, we choose the one that is identical to the noun or the one that is shorter in length.

of ENTITY (which will include PHYSICAL ENTITY and ABSTRACT ENTITY).[3]

4 Experimental Setup

4.1 Corpus and Experimental Expressions

We use the British National Corpus (BNC),[4] automatically parsed using the Collins parser (Collins, 1999), and further processed with TGrep2.[5] We select our potential experimental expressions from pairs of verb and direct object that have a minimum frequency of 25 in the BNC and that involve one of a predefined list of basic (transitive) verbs. Basic verbs, which in their literal uses refer to states or acts central to human experience (e.g., *give* and *put*), commonly form MWEs in combination with their direct object argument (Cowie et al., 1983). We use 12 such verbs ranked highly according to the number of different nouns they appear with in the BNC. Here are the verbs in alphabetical order:

bring, find, get, give, hold, keep, lose, make, put, see, set, take

To guarantee that the final set of expressions contains pairs from all four classes, we pseudo-randomly select them from the initial list of pairs extracted from the BNC as explained above. To ensure the inclusion of IDMs, we consult two idioms dictionaries (Cowie et al., 1983; Seaton and Macaulay, 2002). To ensure we include LVCs, we select pairs in which the noun has a morphologically related verb according to WordNet. We also select pairs whose noun is not morphologically related to any verb to ensure the inclusion of LIT combinations.

This selection process resulted in 632 pairs, reduced to 563 after annotation (see Section 4.2 for details on annotation). Out of these, 148 are LIT, 196 are ABS, 102 are LVC, and 117 are IDM. We randomly choose 102 pairs from each class as our final experimental expressions. We then pseudo-randomly divide these into training (TRAIN), development (DEV), and test (TEST) data sets, so that each set has an equal number of pairs from each class. In addition, we ensure that pairs with the same verb that belong to the same class are divided equally among the three sets. Our final TRAIN, DEV, and TEST sets contain 240, 84, and 84 pairs, respectively.

[3]Experiments on development data show that looking at all senses of a noun degrades performance.

[4]http://www.natcorp.ox.ac.uk.

[5]http://tedlab.mit.edu/~dr/Tgrep2.

4.2 Human Judgments

We asked four native speakers of English with sufficient linguistic background to annotate our experimental expressions. The annotation task was expected to be time-consuming, hence it was not feasible for all the judges to annotate all the expressions. Instead, we asked one judge to be our primary annotator, PA henceforth. (PA is an author of this paper, but the other three judges are not.)

First, PA annotated all the 632 expressions selected as described in Section 4.1, and removed 69 of them that could be potential sources of disagreement for various reasons (e.g., if an expression was unfamiliar or was likely to be part of a larger phrase). Next, we divided the remaining 563 pairs into three equal-sized sets, and gave each set to one of the other judges to annotate. The judges were given a comprehensive guide for the task, in which the classes were defined solely in terms of their semantic properties. Since expressions were annotated out of context (type-based), we asked the judges to annotate the predominant meaning of each expression.

We use the annotations of PA as our gold standard for evaluation, but use the annotations of the others to measure inter-annotator agreement. The observed agreement (p_o) between PA and each of the other three annotators are 79.8%, 72.2%, and 67%, respectively. The kappa (κ) scores are .72, .62, and .56. The reasonably high agreement scores confirm that the classes are coherent and linguistically plausible.

4.3 Classification Strategy and Features

We use the decision tree induction system C5.0 as our machine learning software, and the measures proposed in Section 3 as features in our classification experiments.[6] We explore the relevance of each feature group in the overall classification, as well as in identifying members of each individual class.

5 Experimental Results

We performed experiments on DEV to find features most relevant for classification. These experiments

[6]Experiments on DEV using a Support Vector Machine algorithm produced poorer results; we thus do not report them.

revealed that removing $\mathrm{Sim}_{\mathrm{dist}}(t, v)$ resulted in better performance. This is not surprising given that basic verbs are highly polysemous, and hence the distributional context of a basic verb may not correspond to any particular sense of it. We thus remove this feature (from COMP) in experiments on TEST. Results presented here are on the TEST set; those on the DEV set have similar trends. Here, we first look at the overall performance of classification in Section 5.1. Section 5.2 presents the results of classification for the individual classes.

5.1 Overall Classification Performance

Table 3 presents the results of classification—in terms of average accuracy (%Acc) and relative error reduction (%RER)—for the individual feature groups, as well as for all groups combined. The baseline (chance) accuracy is 25% since we have four equal-sized classes in TEST. As can be seen, INST features yield the lowest overall accuracy, around 36%, with a relative error reduction of only 14% over the baseline. This shows that institutionalization, although relevant, is not sufficient for distinguishing among different levels of semantic idiosyncrasy. Interestingly, FIXD features achieve the highest accuracy, 50%, with a relative error reduction of 33%, showing that fixedness is a salient aspect of semantic idiosyncrasy. COMP features achieve reasonably good accuracy, around 40%, though still notably lower than the accuracy of FIXD features. This is especially interesting since much previous research has focused solely on the non-compositionality of MWEs to identify them (McCarthy et al., 2003; Baldwin et al., 2003; Bannard et al., 2003). Our results confirm the relevance of this property, while at the same time revealing its insufficiency. Interestingly, features related to the semantic properties of the constituents, VERB and NSEM, overall perform comparably to the compositionality features. However, a closer look at their performance on the individual classes (see Section 5.2) reveals that, unlike COMP, they are mainly good at identifying items from certain classes. As hypothesized, we achieve the highest performance, an accuracy of 58% and a relative error reduction of 44%, when we combine all features.

Table 4 displays classification performance, when we use all the feature groups except one. These results are more or less consistent with those in Table 3 above, except some differences which we discuss below. Removing FIXD features results in a drastic decrease in performance (10.7%), while the removal of INST and COMP features cause much smaller drops in performance (4.7% and 2.3%, respectively). Here again, we can see that features related to the semantics of the verb and the noun are salient features. Removing either of these results in a substantial decrease in performance—9.5% and 11.9%, respectively—which is comparable to the decrease resulting from removing FIXD features. This is an interesting observation, since VERB and NSEM features, on their own, do not perform nearly as well as FIXD features. It is thus necessary to futher investigate the performance of these groups on larger data sets with more variability in the verb and noun constituents of the expressions.

Only the features in group	%Acc	(%RER)
INST	35.7	(14.3)
FIXD	50	(33.3)
COMP	40.5	(20.7)
VERB	42.9	(23.9)
NSEM	39.3	(19.1)
ALL	**58.3**	**(44.4)**

Table 3: Accuracy (%Acc) and relative error reduction (%RER) over TEST pairs, for the individual feature groups, and for all features combined.

All features except those in group	%Acc	(%RER)
INST	53.6	(38.1)
FIXD	47.6	(30.1)
COMP	56	(41.3)
VERB	48.8	(31.7)
NSEM	46.4	(28.5)
ALL	**58.3**	**(44.4)**

Table 4: Accuracy (%Acc) and relative error reduction (%RER) over TEST pairs, removing one feature group at a time.

5.2 Performance on Individual Classes

We now look at the performance of the feature groups, both separately and combined, on the individual classes. For each combination of class and feature group, the F-measures of classification are given in Table 5, with the two highest F-measures for each class shown in boldface.[7] These results show that the combination of all feature groups yields the best or the second-best performance on all four classes. (In fact, in only one case is the performance

[7]Our F-measure gives equal weights to precision and recall.

	Only the features in group					
Class	INST	FIXD	COMP	VERB	NSEM	ALL
LIT	.48	.42	.51	.54	**.57**	**.60**
ABS	.40	.32	.17	.27	**.49**	**.46**
LVC	.21	**.58**	.47	.55	-	**.68**
IDM	.33	**.67**	.42	0	-	**.56**

Table 5: F-measures on TEST pairs, for individual feature groups and all features combined.

	ANNOTATOR1		ANNOTATOR2		ANNOTATOR3	
Class	$\%p_o$	κ	$\%p_o$	κ	$\%p_o$	κ
LIT	93.6	.83	88.3	.67	91.4	.78
ABS	83	.63	76.6	.46	78	.52
LVC	91	.71	83	.54	87.7	.61
IDM	92	.73	87.2	.63	87.2	.59

Table 6: Per-class observed agreement and kappa score between PA and each of the three annotators.

of ALL features notably smaller than the best performance achieved by a single feature group.)

Looking at the performance of ALL features, we can see that we get reasonably high F-measure for all classes, except for ABS. The relatively low values of p_o and κ on this class, as shown in Table 6, suggest that this class was also the hardest to annotate. It is possible that members of this class share properties with other classes. The extremely poor performance of the COMP features on ABS also reflects that perhaps members of this class are not coherent in terms of their degree of compositionality (e.g, compare *give confidence* and *make a living*). In the future, we need to incorporate more coherent membership criteria for this class into our annotation procedure.

According to Table 5, the most relevant feature group for identifying members of the LIT and ABS classes is NSEM. This is expected since NSEM is a binary feature determining whether the noun is a PHYSICAL ENTITY or an ABSTRACT ENTITY.[8] Among other feature groups, INST features also perform reasonably well on both these classes. The most relevant feature group for LVC and IDM is FIXD. (Note that for IDM, the performance of this group is notably higher than ALL). On the other hand, INST features have a very poor performance on these classes, reinforcing that IDMs and LVCs may not necessarily appear with significantly high frequency of occurrence in a given corpus. Fixedness features thus prove to be particularly important for the identification of highly idiosyncratic MWEs, such as LVCs and IDMs.

[8]Since this is a binary feature, it can only distinguish two classes. In the future, we need to include more semantic classes.

6 Related Work

Much recent work on classifying MWEs focuses on determining different levels of compositionality in verb+particle combinations using a measure of distributional similarity (McCarthy et al., 2003; Baldwin et al., 2003; Bannard et al., 2003). Another group of research attempts to classify a particular MWE subtype, such as verb-particle constructions (VPCs) or LVCs, according to some fine-grained semantic criteria (Wanner, 2004; Uchiyama et al., 2005; Cook and Stevenson, 2006). Here, we distinguish subtypes of MWEs that are defined according to coarse-grained distinctions in their degree of semantic idiosyncrasy.

Wermter and Hahn (2004) recognize the importance of distinguishing MWE subtypes that are similar to our four classes, but only focus on separating MWEs as one single class from literal combinations. For this, they use a measure that draws on the limited modifiability of MWEs, in addition to their expected high frequency. Krenn and Evert (2001) attempt to separate German idioms, LVCs, and literal phrases (of the form verb+prepositional phrase). They treat LVCs and idioms as institutionalized expressions, and use frequency and several association measures, such as PMI, for the task. The main goal of their work is to find which association measures are particularly suited for identifying which of these classes. Here, we look at properties of MWEs other than their institutionalization (the latter we quantify using an association measure).

The work most similar to ours is that of Venkatapathy and Joshi (2005). They propose a minimally-supervised classification schema that incorporates a variety of features to group verb+noun combinations according to their level of compositionality. Their work has the advantage of requiring only a small amount of manually-labeled training data. However, their classes are defined on the basis of compositionality only. Here, we consider classes that are linguistically salient, and moreover need special treatment within a computational system. Our work is also different in that it brings in a new group of features, the fixedness measures, which prove to be very effective in identifying particular classes of MWEs.

7 Conclusions

We have provided an analysis of the important characteristics pertaining to the semantic idiosyncrasy of MWEs. We have also elaborated on the relationship between these properties and four linguistically-motivated classes of verb+noun combinations, falling on a continuum from less to more semantically idiosyncratic. On the basis of such analysis, we have developed statistical, corpus-based measures that quantify each of these properties. Our results confirm that these measures are effective in type classification of the MWEs under study. Our class-based results look into the interaction between the measures (each capturing a property of MWEs) and the classes (which are defined in terms of semantic idiosyncrasy). Based on this, we can see which measures—or properties they relate to—are most or least relevant for identifying each particular class of verb+noun combinations. We are currently expanding this work to investigate the use of similar measures in token classification of verb+noun combinations in context.

Acknowledgements

We thank Eric Joanis for providing us with NP-head extraction software. We thank Saif Mohammad for the CooccurrenceMatrix and the DistributionalDistance packages.

References

Timothy Baldwin, Colin Bannard, Takaaki Tanaka, and Dominic Widdows. 2003. An empirical model of multiword expression decomposability. In *Proc. of ACL-SIGLEX Wkshp. on Multiword Expressions*, 89–96.

Colin Bannard, Timothy Baldwin, and Alex Lascarides. 2003. A statistical approach to the semantics of verb-particles. In *Proc. of ACL-SIGLEX Wkshp. on Multiword Expressions*, 65–72.

Laurel J. Brinton and Minoji Akimoto, eds. 1999. *Collocational and Idiomatic Aspects of Composite Predicates in the History of English*. John Benjamins.

Miriam Butt. 2003. The light verb jungle. Workshop on Multi-Verb Constructions.

Cristina Cacciari and Patrizia Tabossi, eds. 1993. *Idioms: Processing, Structure, and Interpretation*. Lawrence Erlbaum Associates, Publishers.

Kenneth Church, William Gale, Patrick Hanks, and Donald Hindle. 1991. Using statistics in lexical analysis. In Uri Zernik, editor, *Lexical Acquisition: Exploiting On-Line Resources to Build a Lexicon*, 115–164.

Michael Collins. 1999. *Head-Driven Statistical Models for Natural Language Parsing*. Ph.D. thesis, UPenn.

Paul Cook and Suzanne Stevenson. 2006. Classifying particle semantics in English verb-particle constructions. In *Proc. of COLING-ACL'06 Wkshp. on Multiword Expressions*, 45–53.

Anthony P. Cowie, Ronald Mackin, and Isabel R. McCaig. 1983. *Oxford Dictionary of Current Idiomatic English*, volume 2. OUP.

Anthony P. Cowie. 1981. The treatment of collocations and idioms in learner's dictionaries. *Applied Linguistics*, II(3):223–235.

Afsaneh Fazly and Suzanne Stevenson. 2006. Automatically constructing a lexicon of verb phrase idiomatic combinations. In *Proc. of EACL'06*, 337–344.

Christiane Fellbaum, editor. 1998. *WordNet, An Electronic Lexical Database*. MIT Press.

Raymond W., Jr. Gibbs and Nandini P. Nayak. 1989. Psycholinguistic studies on the syntactic behaviour of idioms. *Cognitive Psychology*, 21:100–138.

Brigitte Krenn and Stefan Evert. 2001. Can we do better than frequency? A case study on extracting PP-verb collocations. In *Proc. of ACL'01 Wkshp. on Collocations*, 39–46.

Dekang Lin. 1998. Automatic retrieval and clustering of similar words. In *Proc. of COLING-ACL'98*, 768–774.

Dekang Lin. 1999. Automatic identification of non-compositional phrases. In *Proc. of ACL'99*, 317–324.

Diana McCarthy, Bill Keller, and John Carroll. 2003. Detecting a continuum of compositionality in phrasal verbs. In *Proc. of ACL-SIGLEX Wkshp. on Multiword Expressions*, 73–80.

Tadao Miyamoto. 2000. *The Light Verb Construction in Japanese: the Role of the Verbal Noun*. John Benjamins.

Rosamund Moon. 1998. *Fixed Expressions and Idioms in English: A Corpus-Based Approach*. Oxford University Press.

Geoffrey Nunberg, Ivan A. Sag, and Thomas Wasow. 1994. Idioms. *Language*, 70(3):491–538.

Ivan A. Sag, Timothy Baldwin, Francis Bond, Ann Copestake, and Dan Flickinger. 2002. Multiword expressions: A pain in the neck for NLP. In *Proc. of CICLing'02*, 1–15.

Maggie Seaton and Alison Macaulay, eds. 2002. *Collins COBUILD Idioms Dictionary*. HarperCollins.

Kiyoko Uchiyama, Timothy Baldwin, and Shun Ishizaki. 2005. Disambiguating Japanese compound verbs. *Computer Speech and Language*, 19:497–512.

Sriram Venkatapathy and Aravind Joshi. 2005. Measuring the relative compositionality of verb-noun (V-N) collocations by integrating features. In *Proc. of HLT-EMNLP'05*, 899–906.

Leo Wanner. 2004. Towards automatic fine-grained semantic classification of verb-noun collocations. *Natural Language Engineering*, 10(2):95–143.

Joachim Wermter and Udo Hahn. 2004. Collocation extraction based on modifiability statistics. In *Proc. of COLING'04*, 980–986.

Design and Implementation of a Lexicon of Dutch Multiword Expressions

Nicole Grégoire
Uil-OTS
University of Utrecht
Utrecht, The Netherlands
Nicole.Gregoire@let.uu.nl

Abstract

This paper describes the design and implementation of a lexicon of Dutch multiword expressions (MWEs). No exhaustive research on a standard lexical representation of MWEs has been done for Dutch before. The approach taken is innovative, since it is based on the Equivalence Class Method. Furthermore, the selection of the lexical entries and their properties is corpus-based. The design of the lexicon and the standard representation will be tested in Dutch NLP systems. The purpose of the current paper is to give an overview of the decisions made in order to come to a standard lexical representation and to discuss the description fields this representation comprises.

1 Introduction

This paper describes the design and implementation of a lexicon of Dutch multiword expressions (MWEs). MWEs are known to be problematic for natural language processing. A considerable amount of research has been conducted in this area. Most progress has been made especially in the field of multiword identification (Villada Moirón and Tiedemann, 2006; Katz and Giesbrecht, 2006; Zhang et al., 2006). Moreover, interesting papers have been written on the representation of MWEs, most of them focusing on a single class of MWEs, see section 2. This paper elaborates on a standard lexical representation for Dutch MWEs developed within the STEVIN IRME project.[1] Part of the project focused on the design and implementation of an electronic resource of 5,000 Dutch expressions that meets the criterion of being highly theory- and implementation-independent, and which can be used in various Dutch NLP systems. The selection of the lexical entries and their properties is corpus-based.

Work has been conducted on collecting Dutch MWEs in the past, yielding one commercial printed dictionary (de Groot, 1999), and an electronic resource called the *Referentiebestand Nederlands* ('Reference Database of The Dutch Language') (Martin and Maks, 2005), both mainly meant for human users. No focus had been put on creating a standard representation for Dutch MWEs that can be converted into any system specific representation. The approach taken is innovative, since it is based on the Equivalence Class Method (ECM) (Odijk, 2004b). The idea behind the ECM is that MWEs that have the same pattern require the same treatment in an NLP system. MWEs with the same pattern form so-called Equivalence Classes (ECs). Having the ECs, it requires some manual work to convert one instance of an EC into a system specific representation, but all other members of the same EC can be done in a fully automatic manner. This method is really powerful since very detailed pattern descriptions can be used for describing the characteristics of a group of MWEs. Besides the description of the MWE patterns, we designed a uniform representation for the description of the individual expressions. Both the pattern descriptions and the MWE descriptions are implemented in the *Lexicon*

[1] http://www-uilots.let.uu.nl/irme/

Proceedings of the Workshop on A Broader Perspective on Multiword Expressions, pages 17–24,
Prague, June 2007.

of Dutch MWEs.

The purpose of this paper is to give an overview of the decisions made in order to come to a standard lexical representation and furthermore to discuss the description fields that are part of this representation.

The paper starts with an overview of related research in section 2. This is followed by elaborating the *Lexicon of Dutch MWEs* in section 3, a discussion in section 4, and a conclusion in section 5.

2 Related research: classes and representations

The area of multiword expressions includes many different subtypes, varying from fixed expressions to syntactically more flexible expressions. Sag et al. (2001) wrote a well-known paper on subclasses of MWEs, in which they make a distinction between *lexicalized phrases* and *institutionalized phrases*. Lexicalized phrases are subdivided into fixed, semi-fixed and flexible expressions. The most important reason for this subdivision is the variation in the degree of syntactic flexibility of MWEs. Roughly they claim that syntactic flexibility is related to semantic decomposability. Semantically non-decomposable idioms are idioms the meaning of which cannot be distributed over its parts and which are therefore not subject to syntactic variability. Sag et al. state that "the only types of lexical variation observable in non-decomposable idioms are inflection (*kicked the bucket*) and variation in reflexive form (*wet oneself*)." Examples of non-decomposable idioms are the oft-cited *kick the bucket* and *shoot the breeze*. On the contrary, semantically decomposable idioms, such as *spill the beans*, tend to be syntactically flexible to some degree. Mapping the boundaries of flexibility, however, is not always easy and no one can predict exactly which types of syntactic variation a given idiom can undergo.

One subtype of flexible expressions discussed in Sag et al. (2001) is the type of *Light Verb Constructions* (or *Support Verb Constructions* (SVCs)). SVCs are combinations of a verb that seems to have very little semantic content and a prepositional phrase, a noun phrase or adjectival phrase. An SVC is often paraphrasable by means of a single verb or adjective. Since the complement of the verb is used in its normal sense, the constructions are subject to standard grammar rules, which include passivization, internal modification, etc. The lexical selection of the verb is highly restricted. Examples of SVCs are *give/*make a demo*, *make/*do a mistake*.

As stated, no exhaustive research on a standard representation of MWEs has been done for Dutch before. Work on this topic has been conducted for other languages, which in most cases focused on a single subtype. Both Dormeyer and Fischer (1998) and Fellbaum et al. (2006) report on work on a resource for German verbal idioms, while the representation of German PP-verb collocations is addressed in (Krenn, 2000). Kuiper et al. (2003) worked on a representation of English idioms, and Villavicencio et al. (2004) proposed a lexical encoding of MWEs in general, by analysing English idioms and verb-partical constructions. Except for the SAID-database (Kuiper et al., 2003), which comprises over 13,000 expression, the created resources contain no more than 1,000 high-frequent expressions. Both Fellbaum et al. and Krenn support their lexical annotation with a corpus-based investigation. In our approach, we also use data extracted from corpora as empirical material, see section 3.2.

In most resources addressed, some kind of syntactic analysis is assigned to individual expressions. The most sophisticated syntactic analysis is done in the SAID-database. The approach taken by Kuiper et al. (2003) would have been more theory-independent, if it included a textual description, according to which classes of idioms could be formed. Villavicencio et al. (2004) defined a specific meta-type for each particular class of MWEs. The meta-types can be used to map the semantic relations between the components of an MWE into grammar specific features. Examples of meta-types specified are *verb-object-idiom* and *verb-particle-np*. They state that the majority of the MWEs in their database could be described by the meta-types defined. But since only a sample of 125 verbal idioms was used for the classification, no estimation can be given of how many classes this approach yields, when consulting a larger set of various types of MWEs. Fellbaum et al. (2006) provide a dependency structure for each expression, but not with the intention of grouping the entries accordingly.

To conclude this section, although our approach is in line with some of the projects described, our work is also distinctive because (1) it focuses on Dutch; (2) it does not solely focus on one type of MWEs, but on MWEs in general; (3) the lexicon includes 5,000 unique expressions, and (4) for an initial version of the lexicon a conversion to the Dutch NLP system Alpino[2] has been tested. In the remainder of this paper we discuss our approach to the lexical representation of MWEs.

3 A Lexicon of Dutch MWEs

In our research multiword expressions are defined as a combination of words that has linguistic properties not predictable from the individual components or the normal way they are combined (Odijk, 2004a). The linguistic properties can be of any type, e.g. *in line* is an MWE according to its syntactic characteristics, since it lacks a determiner preceding the singular count noun *line*, which is obligatory in standard English grammar.

Various aspects played a role in the representation as it is in the *Lexicon of Dutch MWEs*. First of all, the main requirement of the standard encoding is that it can be converted into any system specific representation with a minimal amount of manual work. The method adopted to achieve this goal is the Equivalence Class Method (ECM) (Odijk, 2004b). As stated, the ECM is based on the idea that given a class of MWE descriptions, representations for a specific theory and implementation can be derived. The procedure is that one instance of an Equivalence Class (EC) must be converted manually. By defining and formalizing the conversion procedure, the other instances of the same EC can be converted in a fully automatic manner. In other words, having the ECs consisting of MWEs with the same pattern, it requires some manual work to convert one instance of each EC into a system specific representation, but all other members of the same EC can be done fully automatically. In the current approach, a formal representation of the patterns has been added to the pattern descriptions. Since this formal representation is in agreement with a de facto standard for Dutch (van Noord et al., 2006), most Dutch NLP systems are able to use it for the conversion procedure, yielding an optimal reduction of manual labor.

The creation of MWE descriptions is a very time-consuming task and of course we aim at an error-free result. Accordingly, we decided to describe the minimal ingredients of an MWE that are needed for successful incorporation in any Dutch NLP system. For the development of the representation two Dutch parsers are consulted, viz. the Alpino parser and the Rosetta MT system (Rosetta, 1994).

Another requirement of the lexicon structure is that the information needed for the representation is extractable from corpora, since we want to avoid analyses entirely based on speaker-specific intuitions.

3.1 Subclasses

Each MWE in the lexicon is classified as either fixed, semi-flexible or flexible. In general, our classification conforms to the categorization given in Sag et al. (2001), any differences are explicitly discussed below.

3.1.1 Fixed MWEs

Fixed MWEs always occur in the same word order and there is no variation in lexical item choice. Fixed MWEs cannot undergo morpho-syntactic variation and are contiguous, i.e. no other elements can intervene between the words that are part of the fixed MWE. Examples of Dutch fixed MWEs are: *ad hoc*, *ter plaatse* 'on the spot', *van hoger hand* 'from higher authority'.

3.1.2 Semi-flexible MWEs

The following characteristics are applicable to the class of semi-flexible MWEs in our lexicon:

1. The lexical item selection of the elements of the expression is fixed or very limited.
2. The expression can only be modified as a whole.[3]
3. The individual components can inflect, unless explicitly marked otherwise with a parameter.

Examples of Dutch semi-flexible MWEs are: *de plaat poetsen* (lit. 'to polish the plate', id. 'to clear off'), *witte wijn* 'white wine', *bijvoeglijk naamwoord* 'adjective'.

[2]http://odur.let.rug.nl/~vannoord/alp.

[3]We abstract away from the reason why some external modifiers, such a *proverbial* in *he kicked the proverbial bucket*, may intrude in these semi-flexible expressions.

The characteristics of this class differ on one point from the characteristics of the semi-fixed class discussed in Sag et al. (2001), viz. on the fact that according to Sag et al. semi-fixed expressions are not subject to syntactic variability and the only types of lexical variation are inflection and variation in the reflexive form. This degree of fixedness does not apply to our class of semi-flexible MWEs, i.e. in Dutch (and also in other Germanic languages like German), operations that involve movement of the verb such as verb second, verb first and verb raising, see (1)-(3), are also applicable to the class of semi-flexible expressions (Schenk, 1994).

(1) Hij poetste de plaat.
he polished the plate
'He cleared off.'

(2) Poetste hij the plaat?
polished he the plate
'Did he clear off?'

(3) ... omdat hij de plaat wilde poetsen.
... because he the plate wanted polish
'... because he wanted to clear off'

3.1.3 Flexible MWEs

The main characteristic of flexible MWEs is the fact that, contrary to semi-flexible MWEs, the individual components within flexible MWEs can be modified. This contrast accounts for differences between *de plaat poetsen* versus *een bok schieten* (lit. 'to shoot a male-goat', id. ' to make a blunder') and *blunder maken/begaan* (' to make a blunder'). Although both *een bok schieten* and *blunder maken/begaan* are flexible MWEs, there is a difference between the two expressions. According to the classification proposed by Sag et al. (2001), *een bok schieten* is a decomposable idiom, of which the individual components cannot occur independently in their idiomatic meaning and *een blunder maken* is a support verb construction. We also want to use this classification, and represent these expressions as follows:

1. Expressions of which one part is lexically fixed and the other part is selected from a list of one or more co-occuring lexemes. Dutch examples are: *scherpe/stevige kritiek* ('severe criticism'), *blunder maken/begaan*.
2. Expressions of which the lexical realization of each component consists of exactly one lexeme. A Dutch example is *een bok schieten*.

The difference between the two subtypes is made visible in the representation of the MWE and the MWE pattern.

3.2 The data

We use data extracted from the Twente Nieuws Corpus (TwNC) (Ordelman, 2002) as empirical material.[4] This corpus comprises a 500 million words of newspaper text and television news reports. From the TwNC, a list of candidate expressions is extracted, including for each expression the following properties:

- the pattern assigned to the expression by the Alpino parser
- the frequency
- the head of the expression
- the ten most occurring subjects
- internal complements and for each complement: its head, the head of the complement of the head (in the case of PP complements), its dependency label assigned by Alpino, the number of the noun, whether the noun is positive of diminutive, the ten most occurring determiners, the ten most occurring premodifiers, and the ten most occurring postmodifiers.
- six examples sentences

The use of corpora is necessary but not sufficient. It is necessary because we want our lexicon to reflect actual language usage and because we do not want to restrict ourselves to a linguist's imagination of which uses are possible or actually occur. On the other hand, using the corpora to extract the MWEs is not sufficient for the following reasons: (1) text corpora may contain erroneous usage, and the technique used cannot distinguish this from correct usage; (2) the extraction is in part based on an automatic syntactic parse of the corpus sentences, and these parses may be incorrect; (3) the

[4] The identification of MWEs is done by Begoña Villada Moirón working at the University of Groningen.

extraction techniques cannot distinguish idiomatic versus literal uses of word combinations; (4) the extraction techniques group different expressions that share some but not all words together. Therefore the data extracted were carefully analyzed before creating entries for MWEs.

3.3 The lexical represention

3.3.1 Pattern description

In the *Lexicon of Dutch MWEs*, expressions are classified according to their pattern. In the original ECM the pattern is an identifier which refers to the structure of the idiom represented as free text in which the uniqueness of the pattern is described. This description includes the syntactic category of the head of the expression, the complements it takes and the description of the internal structure of the complements. Furthermore it is described whether individual components can be modified. In the current approach the description of the pattern contains besides a textual description also a formal notation, see (4).

(4) Expressions headed by a verb, taking a fixed direct object constisting of a determiner and a noun – [.VP [.obj1:NP [.det:D (1)] [.hd:N (2)]] [.hd:V (3)]]

The notation used to describe the patterns is a formalization of dependency trees, in particular CGN (*Corpus Gesproken Nederlands* 'Corpus of Spoken Dutch') dependency trees (Hoekstra et al., 2003). CGN dependency structures are based on traditional syntactic analysis described in the Algemene Nederlandse Spraakkunst (Haeseryn et al., 1997) and are aimed to be as theory neutral as possible.

The patterns are encoded using a formal language, which is short and which allows easy visualization of dependency trees. The dependency labels (in lower case) and category labels (in upper case) are divided by a colon (:), e.g. *obj1:NP*. For leaf nodes, the part-of-speech is represented instead of the category label. Leaf nodes are followed by an index that refers to the MWE component as represented in the CL-field (see section 3.3.2), e.g. (1) refers to the first component of the CL, (2) to the second, etc.

A fixed expression can be represented in two ways depending on its internal structure:

1. For fixed expressions that are difficult to assign an internal structure, we introduced a label *fixed*. The pattern for expressions such as *ad hoc* and *ter plaatste* is [.:Adv fixed(1 2)]

2. Fixed expressions with an analyzable internal structure are represented according to the normal pattern description rules:

(5) *de volle buit* ('everything')
[.NP [.det:D (1)] [.mod:A (2)] [.hd:N (3)]]

Semi-flexible MWEs are also represented according to normal pattern description rules. To make a distinction between (1) an NP of which all elements are fixed, and (2) an NP of which some elements are lexically fixed, but which is still subject to standard grammar rules, a new syntactic category *N1* has been introduced. N1 indicates that the expression can be modified as a whole and can take a determiner as specifier:

(6) *witte wijn*
[.N1 [.mod:A (1)] [.hd:N (2)]]

The pattern of flexible expressions of which the lexical realization of each component consists of exactly one lexeme is encoded using the syntactic category N1. We can use the same category as in (6), since what we want to describe is the fact that the components in the NP are fixed, but can be modified as a whole and can take a determiner as specifier.

(7) *bok schieten*
[.VP [.obj1:N1 [.hd:N (1)]] [.hd:V (2)]]

Expressions of which one part is fixed and the other part is selected from a list of one or more co-occuring lexemes are represented with a so-called LIST-index in the pattern. The fixed part of the expression has its literal sense. The combination of the literal part with other lexemes is not predicable from the meaning of the combining lexeme. Since the meaning of an MWE or its parts is not included in the representation, we can list every single component with which the fixed part can combine in the same MWE entry. For this list of components we created a LISTA-field and LISTB-field in the MWE description. Lists and variables are represented similar to MWE components, attached to the leaf node, in lower case and between (), e.g. [.hd:X (list)], [obj1:NP (var)], [obj2:NP (var)], etc.:

(8) *iemand de helpende hand bieden* (lit. 'offer s.o. the helping hand', id. 'lend s.o. a hand') [.VP [.obj2:NP (var)] [.obj1:NP [.det:D (1)] [.mod:A (2)] [.hd:N (3)]] [.hd:V (4)]]

Our characterization of the classes of MWEs and the formal notation of the patterns do not fully cover the range of different types of MWEs that are described in the lexicon. The strength of the ECM is, however, that any expression can be included in the lexicon, regardless of whether it fits our classification, because of the textual description that can be assigned. Expressions that cannot be assigned a dependency structure, because of the limitations of the notation, are classified according to the textual description of its pattern. A revision of the formal notation might be done in the future.

The pattern is part of the MWE pattern description which includes, besides a pattern name, a pattern and a textual description, five additional fields, which are both maintenance field and fields needed for a successful implementation of the standard representation into a system specific representation. Examples of MWE pattern descriptions stored in the *Lexicon of Dutch MWEs* are given in Table 1.

3.3.2 MWE description

In addition to the MWE pattern descriptions, the lexicon contains MWE descriptions, see Table 2 for a list of examples. An MWE description comprises 8 description fields. The PATTERN_NAME is used to assign an MWE pattern description to the expression. The EXPRESSION-field contains the obligatory fixed components of an MWE in the full form.

The Component List (CL) contains the same components as the EXPRESSION-field. The difference is that the components in the CL are in the canonical (or non-inflected) form, instead of in the full form. Parameters are used to specify the full form characteristics of each component. The term *parameter* is a feature and can be defined as an occurrence of the pair <parameter category,parameter value>, where *parameter category* refers to the aspect we parameterize, and *parameter value* to the value a parameter category takes. Examples of parameters are <nnum,sg> for singular nouns, <afrm,sup> for superlative adjectives, <vfrm,part> for particle verbs (Grégoire, 2006). Parameter values are realized between square brackets directly on the right of the item they parameterize.

The LISTA-field and LISTB-field are used to store components that can be substituted for the LIST-index in the pattern, yielding one or more expressions. The reason for using two LIST-fields is to separate predefined list values from special list values. The predefined list values are high frequent verbs that are known to occur often as so-called light verbs, especially with PPs. Two sets of verbs are predefined:

1. blijken ('appear') blijven ('remain') gaan ('go') komen ('come') lijken ('appear') raken ('get') schijnen ('seem') vallen ('be') worden ('become') zijn ('be')

2. brengen ('bring') doen ('do') geven ('give') hebben ('have') houden ('keep') krijgen ('get') maken ('make') zetten ('put')

A complement co-occurs either with verbs from set 1 or with verbs from set 2. Each verb from the chosen set is checked against the occurrences found in the corpus data. If a verb does not occur in the corpus data and also not in self-constructed data, it is deleted from the LISTA-field. The LISTB-field contains lexemes that are not in the predefined set but do co-occur with the component(s) in the EXPRESSION-field. The information in the LISTB-field is merely based on corpus data and therefore may not be exhaustive.

The EXAMPLE-field contains an example sentence with the expression. The only requirement of this field is that its structure is identical for each expression with the same PATTERN_NAME. The POLARITY-field is *none* by default and takes the value *NPI* if an expression can only occur in negative environments, and *PPI* if an expression can only occur in positive environments. Finally, the MWE description contains a field with a reference to a plain text file in which the information extracted from the corpora is stored.

4 Discussion

We have given an overview of the decisions made in order to come to a standard lexical representation for Dutch MWEs and discussed the description

NAME	PATTERN	DESCRIPTION
EC1	[.VP [.obj1:NP [.det:D (1)] [.hd:N (2)]] [.hd:V (3)]]	Expressions headed by a verb, taking a fixed direct object contisting of a determiner and a noun.
EC2	[.VP [.obj1:N1 [.hd:N (1)]] [.hd:V (list)]]	Expressions headed by a verb, taking a direct object consisting of a fixed modifiable and inflectable noun (list).
EC9	[.VP [.obj1:N1 [.hd:N (1)]] [.hd:V (list)] [.pc:PP [.hd:P (2)] [obj1:NP (var)]]]	Expressions headed by a verb, taking (1) a direct object consisting of a fixed modifiable noun, and (2) a PP-argument consisting of a fixed preposition and a variable complement (list).

Table 1: List of MWE pattern descriptions.

PATTERN	EXPRESSION	CL	LIST
EC1	zijn kansen waarnemen ('to seize the opportunity')	zijn kans[pl] waarnemen	-
EC2	blunder ('mistake')	blunder	begaan ('commit') maken ('make')
EC9	kans op ('to stand a change of s.th.')	kans op	lopen ('get') maken

Table 2: List of MWE descriptions.

fields this representation comprises. Contrary to related work, we did not solely focus on one type of MWEs, but on MWEs in general. The *Lexicon of Dutch MWEs* includes 5,000 unique expressions and for an initial version a conversion to the Dutch NLP system Alpino has been tested. The strength of our method lies in the ability of grouping individual expressions according to their pattern, yielding multiple classes of MWEs. The advantage of creating classes of MWEs is that it eases the conversion of the standard representation into any system specific representation.

Describing a class of MWEs using free text is already very useful in its current form. To help speeding up the process of converting the standard representation into a system specific representation, we introduced a formal notation using dependency structures, which are aimed to be as theory neutral as possible. However, our current notation is unable to cover all the patterns described in the lexicon. The notation can be extended, but we must make sure that it does not become too ad hoc and more complicated than interpreting free text.

We have created a resource that is suited for a wide variety of MWEs. The resource describes a set of essential properties for each MWE and classifies each expression as either fixed, semi-flexible or flexible. The set of properties can surely be extended, but we have limited ourselves to a number of core properties because of resource limitations. We are confident that this resource can form a good basis for an even more complete description of MWEs.

5 Conclusion

This paper described the design and implementation of a lexicon of Dutch multiword expressions. No exhaustive research on a standard representation of MWEs has been done for Dutch before. Data extracted form large Dutch text corpora were used as empirical material. The approach taken is innovative, since it is based on the Equivalence Class Method (ECM). The ECM focuses on describing MWEs according to their pattern, making it possible to form classes of MWEs that require the same treatment in natural language processing. The *Lexicon of*

Dutch MWEs constitutes 5,000 unique expressions and for an initial version of the lexicon a conversion to the Dutch NLP system Alpino has been tested.

Acknowledgements

The IRME project is carried out within the STEVIN programme which is funded by the Dutch and Flemish Governments (http://taalunieversum.org/stevin).

The author would like to thank Jan Odijk and two anonymous reviewers for their valuable input to this paper.

References

Hans de Groot. 1999. *Van Dale Idioomwoordenboek*. Van Dale Lexicografie, Utrecht.

Ricarda Dormeyer and Ingrid Fischer. 1998. Building lexicons out of a database for idioms. In Antonio Rubio, Nativiad Gallardo, Rosa Castro, and Antonio Tejada, editors, *Proceedings of the First International Conference on Language Resources and Evaluation*, pages 833 – 838.

Christiane Fellbaum, Alexander Geyken, Axel Herold, Fabian Koerner, and Gerald Neumann. 2006. Corpus-Based Studies of German Idioms and Light Verbs. *International Journal of Lexicography*, 19(4):349–361.

Nicole Grégoire. 2006. Elaborating the parameterized equivalence class method for dutch. In Nicoletta Calzolari, editor, *Proceedings of the Fifth International Conference on Language Resources and Evaluation (LREC 2006)*, pages 1894–99, Genoa, Italy. ELRA.

W. Haeseryn, K. Romijn, G. Geerts, J. de Rooij, and M.C. van den Toorn. 1997. *Algemene Nederlandse Spraakkunst*. Martinus Nijhoff and Wolters Plantyn, Groningen en Deurne.

Heleen Hoekstra, Michael Moortgat, Bram Renmans, Machteld Schouppe, Ineke Schuurman, and Ton van der Wouden. 2003. Cgn syntactische annotatie.

Graham Katz and Eugenie Giesbrecht. 2006. Automatic identification of non-compositional multi-word expressions using latent semantic analysis. In *Proceedings of the ACL 2006 Workshop on Multiword Expressions: Identifying and Exploiting Underlying Properties.*, Sydney, Australia.

Brigitte Krenn. 2000. CDB - a database of lexical collocations. In *2nd International Conference on Language Resources & Evaluation (LREC '00), May 31 - June 2*, Athens, Greece. ELRA.

Koenraad Kuiper, Heather McCann, Heidi Quinn, Therese Aitchison, and Kees van der Veer. 2003. SAID: A syntactically annotated idiom dataset. Linguistic Data Consortium, LDC2003T10, Pennsylvania.

Willy Martin and Isa Maks. 2005. Referentie bestand nederlands documentatie. Technical report, INL.

Jan Odijk. 2004a. Multiword expressions in NLP. Course presentation, LOT Summerschool, Utrecht, July.

Jan Odijk. 2004b. A proposed standard for the lexical representation of idioms. In *EURALEX 2004 Proceedings*, pages 153–164. Université de Bretagne Sud, July.

R.J.F. Ordelman. 2002. Twente nieuws corpus (TwNC).

M T. Rosetta. 1994. *Compositional Translation*. Kluwer Academic Publishers, Dordrecht.

Ivan A. Sag, Timothy Baldwin, Francis Bond, Ann Copestake, and Dan Flickinger. 2001. Multiword expressions: A pain in the neck for NLP. LinGO Working Paper, (2001-03).

André Schenk. 1994. *Idioms and collocations in compositional grammars*. Ph.D. thesis, University of Utrecht.

Gertjan van Noord, Ineke Schuurman, and Vincent Vandeghinste. 2006. Syntactic annotation of large corpora in stevin. In *Proceedings of the Fifth International Conference on Language Resources and Evaluation (LREC 2006)*, Genoa - Italy.

Begona Villada Moirón and Joerg Tiedemann. 2006. Identifying idiomatic expressions using automatic word-alignment. In *Proceedings of the EACL 2006 Workshop on Multiword Expressions in a Multilingual Context*, Trento, Italy.

Aline Villavicencio, Ann Copestake, Benjamin Waldron, and Fabre Lambeau. 2004. The lexical encoding of MWEs. In T. Tanaka, A. Villavicencio, F. Bond, and A. Korhonen, editors, *Proceedings of the ACL 2004 Workshop on Multiword Expressions: Integrating Processing*, Barcelona, Spain.

Yi Zhang, Valia Kordoni, Aline Villavicencio, and Marco Idiart. 2006. Automated multiword expression prediction for grammar engineering. In *Proceedings of the ACL 2006 Workshop on Multiword Expressions: Identifying and Exploiting Underlying Properties.*, Sydney, Australia.

Semantics-based Multiword Expression Extraction

Tim Van de Cruys and Begoña Villada Moirón
Alfa Informatica, University of Groningen
Oude Kijk in 't Jatstraat 26
9712 EK Groningen, The Netherlands
{T.Van.de.Cruys|M.B.Villada.Moiron}@rug.nl

Abstract

This paper describes a fully unsupervised and automated method for large-scale extraction of multiword expressions (MWEs) from large corpora. The method aims at capturing the non-compositionality of MWEs; the intuition is that a noun within a MWE cannot easily be replaced by a semantically similar noun. To implement this intuition, a noun clustering is automatically extracted (using distributional similarity measures), which gives us clusters of semantically related nouns. Next, a number of statistical measures – based on selectional preferences – is developed that formalize the intuition of non-compositionality. Our approach has been tested on Dutch, and automatically evaluated using Dutch lexical resources.

1 Introduction

MWEs are expressions whose linguistic behaviour is not predictable from the linguistic behaviour of their component words. Baldwin (2006) characterizes the idiosyncratic behavior of MWEs as "a lack of compositionality manifest at different levels of analysis, namely, lexical, morphological, syntactic, semantic, pragmatic and statistical". Some MWEs show productive morphology and/or syntactic flexibility. Therefore, these two aspects are not sufficient conditions to discriminate actual MWEs from productive expressions. Nonetheless, the mentioned characteristics are useful indicators to distinguish literal and idiomatic expressions (Fazly and Stevenson, 2006).

One property that seems to affect MWEs the most is semantic non-compositionality. MWEs are typically non-compositional. As a consequence, it is not possible to replace the noun of a MWE by semantically related nouns. Take for example the expressions in (1) and (2):

(1) a. break the vase
b. break the cup
c. break the dish

(2) a. break the ice
b. *break the snow
c. *break the hail

Expression (1-a) is fully compositional. Therefore, *vase* can easily be replaced with semantically related nouns such as *cup* and *dish*. Expression (2-a), on the contrary, is non-compositional; *ice* cannot be replaced with semantically related words, such as *snow* and *hail* without loss of the original meaning.

Due to the idiosyncratic behavior, current proposals argue that MWEs need to be described in the lexicon (Sag et al., 2002). In most languages, electronic lexical resources (such as dictionaries, thesauri, ontologies) suffer from a limited coverage of MWEs. To facilitate the update and expansion of language resources, the NLP community would clearly benefit from automated methods that extract MWEs from large text collections. This is the main motivation to pursue an automated and fully unsupervised MWE extraction method.

Proceedings of the Workshop on A Broader Perspective on Multiword Expressions, pages 25–32,
Prague, June 2007.

2 Previous Work

Recent proposals that attempt to capture semantic compositionality (or lack thereof) employ various strategies. Approaches evaluated so far make use of dictionaries with semantic annotation (Piao et al., 2006), WordNet (Pearce, 2001), automatically generated thesauri (Lin, 1999; McCarthy et al., 2003; Fazly and Stevenson, 2006), vector-based methods that measure semantic distance (Baldwin et al., 2003; Katz and Giesbrecht, 2006), translations extracted from parallel corpora (Villada Moirón and Tiedemann, 2006) or hybrid methods that use machine learning techniques informed by features coded using some of the above methods (Venkatapathy and Joshi, 2005).

Pearce (2001) describes a method to extract collocations from corpora by measuring semantic compositionality. The underlying assumption is that a fully compositional expression allows synonym replacement of its component words, whereas a collocation does not. Pearce measures to what degree a collocation candidate allows synonym replacement. The measurement is used to rank candidates relative to their compositionality.

Building on Lin (1998), McCarthy et al. (2003) measure the semantic similarity between expressions (verb particles) as a whole and their component words (verb). They exploit contextual features and frequency information in order to assess meaning overlap. They established that human compositionality judgements correlate well with those measures that take into account the semantics of the particle. Contrary to these measures, standard association measures poorly correlate with human judgements.

A different approach proposed by Villada Moirón and Tiedemann (2006) measures translational entropy as a sign of meaning predictability, and therefore non-compositionality. The entropy observed among word alignments of a potential MWE varies: highly predictable alignments show less entropy and probably correspond to compositional expressions. Data sparseness and polysemy pose problems because the entropy cannot be accurately calculated.

Fazly and Stevenson (2006) use lexical and syntactic fixedness as partial indicators of non-compositionality. Their method uses Lin's (1998) automatically generated thesaurus to compute a metric of lexical fixedness. Lexical fixedness measures the deviation between the pointwise mutual information of a verb-object phrase and the average pointwise mutual information of the expressions resulting from substituting the noun by its synonyms in the original phrase. This measure is similar to Lin's (1999) proposal for finding non-compositional phrases. Separately, a syntactic flexibility score measures the probability of seeing a candidate in a set of pre-selected syntactic patterns. The assumption is that non-compositional expressions score high in idiomaticity, that is, a score resulting from the combination of lexical fixedness and syntactic flexibility. The authors report an 80% accuracy in distinguishing literal from idiomatic expressions in a test set of 200 expressions. The performance of both metrics is stable across all frequency ranges.

In this study, we are interested in establishing whether a fully unsupervised method can capture the (partial or) non-compositionality of MWEs. The method should not depend on the existence of large (open domain) parallel corpora or sense tagged corpora. Also, the method should not require numerous adjustments when applied to new subclasses of MWEs, for instance, when coding empirical attributes of the candidates. Similar to Lin (1999), McCarthy et al. (2003) and Fazly and Stevenson (2006), our method makes use of automatically generated thesauri; the technique used to compile the thesauri differs from previous work. Aiming at finding a method of general applicability, the measures to capture non-compositionality differ from those employed in earlier work.

3 Methodology

In the description and evaluation of our algorithm, we focus on the extraction of verbal MWEs that contain prepositional complements, although we believe the method can be easily generalized to other kinds of MWEs.

In our semantics-based approach, we want to formalize the intuition of non-compositionality, so that MWE extraction can be done in a fully automated way. A number of statistical measures are developed that try to capture the MWE's non-compositional bond between a verb-preposition combination and its noun by comparing the particular noun of a MWE candidate to other semantically related nouns.

3.1 Data extraction

The MWE candidates (verb + prepositional phrase) are automatically extracted from the *Twente Nieuws Corpus* (Ordelman, 2002), a large corpus of Dutch newspaper texts (500 million words), which has been automatically parsed by the Dutch dependency parser Alpino (van Noord, 2006). Next, a matrix is created of the 5,000 most frequent verb-preposition combinations by the 10,000 most frequent nouns, containing the frequency of each MWE candidate.[1] To this matrix, a number of statistical measures are applied to determine the non-compositionality of the candidate MWEs. These statistical measures are explained in 3.3.

3.2 Clustering

In order to compare a noun to its semantically related nouns, a noun clustering is created. These clusters are automatically extracted using standard distributional similarity techniques (Weeds, 2003; van der Plas and Bouma, 2005). First, dependency triples are extracted from the *Twente Nieuws Corpus*. Next, feature vectors are created for each noun, containing the frequency of the dependency relations in which the noun occurs.[2] This way, a frequency matrix of 10K nouns by 100K dependency relations is constructed. The cell frequencies are replaced by pointwise mutual information scores (Church et al., 1991), so that more informative features get a higher weight. The noun vectors are then clustered into 1,000 clusters using a simple K-means clustering algorithm (MacQueen, 1967) with cosine similarity. During development, several other clustering algorithms and parameters have been tested, but the settings described above gave us the best EuroWordNet similarity score (using Wu and Palmer (1994)).

Note that our clustering algorithm is a hard clustering algorithm, which means that a certain noun can only be assigned to one cluster. This may pose a problem for polysemous nouns. On the other hand, this makes the computation of our metrics straightforward, since we do not have to decide among various senses of a word.

3.3 Measures

The measures used to find MWEs are inspired by Resnik's method to find selectional preferences (Resnik, 1993; Resnik, 1996). Resnik uses a number of measures based on the Kullback-Leibler divergence, to measure the difference between the prior probability of a noun class $p(c)$ and the probability of the class given a verb $p(c|v)$. We adopt the method for particular nouns, and add a measure for determining the 'unique preference' of a noun given other nouns in the cluster, which, we claim, yields a measure of non-compositionality. In total, 4 measures are used, the latter two being the symmetric counterpart of the former two.

The first two measures, $A_{v \to n}$ (equation 2) and $R_{v \to n}$ (equation 3), formalize the unique preference of the verb[3] for the noun. Equation 1 gives the Kullback-Leibler divergence between the overall probability distribution of the nouns and the probability distribution of the nouns given a verb; it is used as a normalization constant in equation 2. Equation 2 models the actual preference of the verb for the noun.

$$S_v = \sum_n p(n \mid v) \, log \frac{p(n \mid v)}{p(n)} \tag{1}$$

$$A_{v \to n} = \frac{p(n \mid v) \, log \frac{p(n|v)}{p(n)}}{S_v} \tag{2}$$

When $p(n|v)$ is 0, $A_{v \to n}$ is undefined. In this case, we assign a score of 0.

Equation 3 gives the ratio of the verb preference for a particular noun, compared to the other nouns that are present in the cluster.

$$R_{v \to n} = \frac{A_{v \to n}}{\sum_{n' \epsilon C} A_{v \to n'}} \tag{3}$$

When $R_{v \to n}$ is more or less equally divided among the different nouns in the cluster, there is no

[1] The lowest frequency verb-preposition combination (with regard to the 10,000 nouns) appears 3 times.

[2] e.g. dependency relations that qualify *apple* might be 'object of *eat*' and 'adjective *red*'. This gives us dependency triples like $< apple, obj, eat >$.

[3] We will use 'verb' to designate a prepositional verb, i.e. a combination of a verb and a preposition.

preference of the verb for a particular noun in the cluster, whereas scores close to 1 indicate a 'unique' preference of the verb for a particular noun in the cluster. Candidates whose $R_{v \to n}$ value approaches 1 are likely to be non-compositional expressions.

In the latter two measures, $A_{n \to v}$ and $R_{n \to v}$, the direction of preference is changed: equations 4 and 5 are the symmetric counterparts of equations 2 and 3. Instead of the preference of the verb for the noun, the preference of the noun for the verb is modelled. Except for the change of preference direction, the characteristics of the former and the latter two measures are the same.

$$A_{n \to v} = \frac{p(v \mid n) \, log \frac{p(v|n)}{p(v)}}{S_n} \quad (4)$$

$$R_{n \to v} = \frac{A_{n \to v}}{\sum_{n' \epsilon C} A_{n' \to v}} \quad (5)$$

Note that, despite their symmetry, the measures for verb preference and the measures for noun preference are different in nature. It is possible that a certain verb only selects a restricted number of nouns, while the nouns themselves can co-occur with many different verbs. This brings about different probability distributions. In our evaluation, we want to investigate the impact of both preferences.

3.4 Example

In this section, an elaborated example is presented, to show how our method works. Take for example the two MWE candidates in (3):

(3) a. in de smaak vallen
in the taste fall
to be appreciated

b. in de put vallen
in the well fall
to fall down the well

In the first expression, *smaak* cannot be replaced with other semantically similar nouns, such as *geur* 'smell' and *zicht* 'sight', whereas in the second expression, *put* can easily be replaced with other semantically similar words, such as *kuil* 'hole' and *krater* 'crater'.

The first step in the formalization of this intuition, is the extraction of the clusters in which the words *smaak* and *put* appear from our clustering database. This gives us the clusters in (4).

(4) a. **smaak**: *aroma* 'aroma', *gehoor* 'hearing', *geur* 'smell', *gezichtsvermogen* 'sight', *reuk* 'smell', *spraak* 'speech', *zicht* 'sight'

b. **put**: *afgrond* 'abyss', *bouwput* 'building excavation', *gaatje* 'hole', *gat* 'hole', *hiaat* 'gap', *hol* 'cave', *kloof* 'gap', *krater* 'crater', *kuil* 'hole', *lacune* 'lacuna', *leemte* 'gap', *valkuil* 'pitfall'

Next, the various measures described in section 3.3 are applied. Resulting scores are given in tables 1 and 2.

MWE candidate	$A_{v \to n}$	$R_{v \to n}$	$A_{n \to v}$	$R_{n \to v}$
val#in smaak	.12	1.00	.04	1.00
val#in geur	.00	.00	.00	.00
val#in zicht	.00	.00	.00	.00

Table 1: Scores for MWE candidate *in de smaak vallen* and other nouns in the same cluster.

Table 1 gives the scores for the MWE *in de smaak vallen*, together with some other nouns that are present in the same cluster. $A_{v \to n}$ shows that there is a clear preference (.12) of the verb *val in* for the noun *smaak*. $R_{v \to n}$ shows that there is a unique preference of the verb for the particular noun *smaak*. For the other nouns (*geur, zicht, ...*), the verb has no preference whatsoever. Therefore, the ratio of verb preference for *smaak* compared to the other nouns in the cluster is 1.00.

$A_{n \to v}$ and $R_{n \to v}$ show similar behaviour. There is a preference (.04) of the noun *smaak* for the verb *val in*, and this preference is unique (1.00).

MWE candidate	$A_{v \to n}$	$R_{v \to n}$	$A_{n \to v}$	$R_{n \to v}$
val#in put	.00	.05	.00	.05
val#in kuil	.01	.11	.02	.37
val#in kloof	.00	.02	.00	.03
val#in gat	.04	.71	.01	.24

Table 2: Scores for MWE candidate *in de put vallen* and other nouns in same cluster.

Table 2 gives the scores for the instance *in de put vallen* – which is not a MWE – together with other nouns from the same cluster. The results are quite different from the ones in table 1. $A_{v \rightarrow n}$ – the preference of the verb for the noun – is quite low in most cases, the highest score being a score of .04 for *gat*. Furthermore, $R_{v \rightarrow n}$ does not show a unique preference of *val in* for *put* (a low ratio score of .05). Instead, the preference mass is divided among the various nouns in the cluster, the highest preference of *val in* being assigned to the noun *gat* (.71).[4]

The other two scores show again a similar tendency; $A_{n \rightarrow v}$ – the preference of the noun for the verb – is low in all cases, and when all nouns in the cluster are considered ($R_{n \rightarrow v}$), there is no 'unique' preference of one noun for the verb *val in*. Instead, the preference mass is divided among all nouns in the cluster.

4 Results & Evaluation

4.1 Quantitative evaluation

In this section, we quantitatively evaluate our method, and compare it to the lexical and syntactic fixedness measures proposed by Fazly and Stevenson (2006). More information about Fazly and Stevenson's measures can be found in their paper.

The potential MWEs that are extracted with the fully unsupervised method described above and with Fazly and Stevenson's (2006) method (FS from here onwards) are automatically evaluated by comparing the extracted list to handcrafted MWE databases. Since we have extracted Dutch MWEs, we are using the two Dutch resources available: the Referentie Bestand Nederlands (RBN, Martin and Maks (2005)) and the Van Dale Lexicographical Information System (VLIS) database. Evaluation scores are calculated with regard to the MWEs that are present in our evaluation resources. Among the MWEs in our reference data, we consider only those expressions that are present in our frequency matrix: if the verb is not among the 5,000 most frequent verbs, or the noun is not among the 10,000 most frequent nouns, the frequency information is not present in our input data. Consequently, our algorithm would never be able to find those MWEs.

The first six rows of table 3 show precision, recall and f-measure for various parameter thresholds with regard to the measures $A_{v \rightarrow n}$, $R_{v \rightarrow n}$, $A_{n \rightarrow v}$ and $R_{n \rightarrow v}$, together with the number of candidates found (n). The last 3 rows show the highest values we were able to reach by using FS's fixedness scores.

Using only two parameters – $A_{v \rightarrow n}$ and $R_{v \rightarrow n}$ – gives the highest f-measure ($\pm$ 14%), with a precision and recall of about 17% and about 12% respectively. Adding parameter $R_{n \rightarrow v}$ increases precision but degrades recall, and this tendency continues when adding both parameters $A_{n \rightarrow v}$ and $R_{n \rightarrow v}$. In all cases, a higher threshold increases precision but degrades recall. When using a high threshold for all parameters, the algorithm is able to reach a precision of $\pm$ 38%, but recall is low ($\pm$ 4%).

Lexical fixedness reaches an f-measure of $\pm$ 12% (threshold of 3.00). These scores show the best performance that we reached using lexical fixedness. Following FS, we evaluated the syntactic fixedness scores of expressions falling above a frequency cutoff. Since our corpus is much larger than that used by FS, a frequency cutoff of 50 was chosen. The precision, recall and f-measure of the syntactic fixedness measure (shown on table 3) are $\pm$ 10%, 41% and 16% respectively, showing worse precision than our method but much better recall and f-measure. As shown by FS, syntactic fixedness performs better than lexical fixedness; $Fixedness_{overall}$ improves on the syntactic fixedness results and also reaches better overall performance than our method.

The compared methods show a different behavior. FS's method favours high recall whereas our method prefers the best trade-off between precision and recall. We wish to highlight that our method reaches better precision than FS's method while handling many low frequency candidates (minimum frequency is 3); this makes our method preferable in some NLP tasks. It is possible that the two methods are capturing different properties of MWEs; in future work, we want to analyse whether the expressions extracted by the two methods differ.

[4] The expression is ambiguous: it can be used in a literal sense (*in een gat vallen*, 'to fall down a hole') and in a metaphorical sense (*in een zwart gat vallen*, 'to get depressed after a joyful or busy period').

parameters					precision	recall	f-measure
$A_{v \to n}$	$R_{v \to n}$	$A_{n \to v}$	$R_{n \to v}$	n	(%)	(%)	(%)
.10	.80	–	–	3175	16.09	13.11	14.45
.10	.90	–	–	2655	17.59	11.98	14.25
.10	.80	–	.80	2225	19.19	10.95	13.95
.10	.90	–	.90	1870	20.70	9.93	13.42
.10	.80	.01	.80	1859	20.33	9.69	13.13
.20	.99	.05	.99	404	38.12	3.95	7.16
$Fixedness_{lex}(v,n)$ 3.00				3899	15.14	9.92	11.99
$Fixedness_{syn}(v,n)$ 50				15,630	10.20	40.90	16.33
$Fixedness_{overall}(v,n)$ 50				7819	13.73	27.54	18.33

Table 3: Evaluation results compared to RBN & VLIS

4.2 Qualitative evaluation

Next, we elaborate upon advantages and disadvantages of our semantics-based MWE extraction algorithm by examining the output of the procedure, and looking at the characteristics of the MWEs found and the errors made by the algorithm.

First of all, our algorithm is able to filter out grammatical collocations that cause problems in traditional MWE extraction paradigms. An example is given in (5).

(5) voldoen aan eisen, voorwaarden
meet to demands, conditions
meet the {demands, conditions}

In traditional MWE extraction algorithms, based on collocations, highly frequent expressions like the ones in (5) often get classified as a MWE, even though they are fully compositional. Such algorithms correctly identify a strong lexical affinity between two component words (*voldoen*, *aan*), which make up a grammatical collocation; however, they fail to capture the fact that the noun may be filled in by a semantic class of nouns. Our algorithm filters out those expressions, because semantic similarity between nouns that fill in the object slot is taken into account.

Our quantitative evaluation shows that the algorithm reaches the best results (i.e. the highest f-measures) when using only two parameters ($A_{v \to n}$ and $R_{v \to n}$). Upon closer inspection of the output, we noticed that $A_{n \to v}$ and $R_{n \to v}$ are often able to filter out non-MWEs like the expressions b in (6) and (7).

(6) a. verschijnen op toneel
appear on stage
to appear

b. zingen op toneel
sing on stage
to sing on the stage

(7) a. lig in geheugen
lie in memory
be in memory

b. lig in ziekenhuis
lie in hospital
lie in the hospital

It is only when the two other measures (a unique preference of the noun for the verb) are taken into account that the b expressions are filtered out – either because the noun preference for the verb is very low, or because it is more evenly distributed among the cluster. The b expressions, which are non-MWEs, result from the combination of a verb with a highly frequent PP. These PPs are typically locative, directional or predicative PPs, that may combine with numerous verbs.

Also, expressions like the ones in (8), where the fixedness of the expression lies not so much in the verb-noun combination, but more in the noun part (*naar school*, *naar huis*) are filtered out by the latter two measures. These preposition-noun combinations seem to be institutionalized PPs, so-called determinerless PPs.

(8) a. naar school willen
to school want
want to go to school

b. naar huis willen
to home want
want to go home

We will now look at some errors made by our algorithm. First of all, our algorithm highly depends on the quality of the noun clustering. If a noun appears in a cluster with unrelated words, the measures will overrate the semantic uniqueness of the expressions in which the noun appears.

Secondly, syntax might play an important role. Sometimes, there are syntactic restrictions between the preposition and the noun. A noun like *pagina* 'page' can only appear with the preposition *op* 'on', as in *lees op pagina* 'read on page'. Other, semantically related nouns, such as *hoofdstuk* 'chapter', prefer *in* 'in'. Due to these restrictions, the measures will again overrate the semantic uniqueness of the noun (*pagina* in the example).

Finally, our hard clustering method does not take polysemous nouns into account. A noun may only occur in one cluster, ignoring other possible meanings. *Schaal*, for example, means 'dish' as well as 'scale'. In our clustering, it only appears in a cluster of dish-related nouns. Therefore, expressions like *maak gebruik op [grote] schaal* 'make use of [sth.] on a [large] scale', receive again overrated measures of semantic uniqueness, because the 'scale' sense of the noun is compared to nouns related to the 'dish' sense.

5 Conclusions and further work

Our algorithm based on non-compositionality explores a new approach aimed at large-scale MWE extraction. Using only two parameters, $A_{v \to n}$ and $R_{v \to n}$, yields the highest f-measure. Using the two other parameters, $A_{n \to v}$ and $R_{n \to v}$, increases precision but degrades recall. Due to the formalization of the intuition of non-compositionality (using an automatic noun clustering), our algorithm is able to rule out various expressions that are coined MWEs by traditional algorithms.

Note that our algorithm has taken on a purely semantics-based approach. 'Syntactic fixedness' of the expressions is not taken into account. Combining our semantics-based approach with other extraction techniques such as the syntactic fixedness measure proposed by Fazly and Stevenson (2006) might improve the results significantly.

We conclude with some issues saved for future work. First of all, we would like to combine our semantics-based method with other methods that are used to find MWEs (especially syntax-based methods), and implement the method in general classification models (decision tree classifier and maximum entropy model). This includes the use of a more principled (machine learning) framework in order to establish the optimal threshold values.

Next, we would like to investigate a number of topics to improve on our semantics-based method. First of all, using the top *k* similar nouns for a certain noun – instead of the cluster in which a noun appears – might be more beneficial to get a grasp of the compositionality of MWE candidates. Also, making use of a verb clustering in addition to the noun clustering might help in determining the non-compositionality of expressions. Disambiguating among the various senses of nouns should also be a useful improvement. Furthermore, we would like to generalize our method to other syntactic patterns (e.g. verb object combinations), and test the approach for English.

One final issue is the realization of a manual evaluation of our semantics-based algorithm, by having human judges decide whether a MWE candidate found by our algorithm is an actual MWE. Our automated evaluation framework is error-prone due to mistakes and incompleteness of our resources. During qualitative evaluation, we found many actual MWEs found by our algorithm, that were not considered correct by our resources (e.g. *[iemand] in de gordijnen jagen* 'to drive s.o. mad', *op het [verkeerde] paard gokken* 'back the wrong horse', *[de kat] uit de boom kijken* 'wait to see which way the wind blows', *uit het [goede] hout gesneden* 'be a trustworthy person'). Conversely, there were also questionable MWE candidates that were described as actual MWEs in our evaluation resources (*val op woensdag* 'fall on a wednesday', *neem als voorzitter* 'take as chairperson', *ruik naar haring* 'smell like herring', *ben voor [...] procent* 'to be ... percent'). A manual evaluation could overcome these difficulties.

We believe that our method provides a genuine

and successful approach to get a grasp of the non-compositionality of MWEs in a fully automated way. We also believe that it is one of the first methods able to extract MWEs based on non-compositionality on a large scale, and that traditional MWE extraction algorithms will benefit from taking this non-compositionality into account.

Acknowledgements

This research was carried out as part of the research program IRME STEVIN project. We would also like to thank Gertjan van Noord and the two anonymous reviewers for their helpful comments on an earlier version of this paper.

References

T. Baldwin, C. Bannard, T. Tanaka, and D. Widdows. 2003. An Empirical Model of Multiword Expressions Decomposability. In *Proc. of the ACL-2003 Workshop on Multiword Expressions: Analysis, Acquisition and Treatment*, pages 89–96, Sapporo, Japan.

T. Baldwin. 2006. Compositionality and Multiword Expressions: Six of One, Half a Dozen of the Other? Invited talk given at the COLING/ACL'06 Workshop on Multiword Expressions: Identifying and Exploiting Underlying Properties, July.

K. Church, W. Gale, P. Hanks, and D. Hindle. 1991. Using statistics in lexical analysis. In Uri Zernik, editor, *Lexical Acquisition: Exploiting On-line resources to build a lexicon*, pages 115–164. Lawrence Erlbaum Associates, New Jersey.

A. Fazly and S. Stevenson. 2006. Automatically constructing a lexicon of verb phrase idiomatic combinations. In *Proceedings of the 11th Conference of the European Chapter of the Association for Computational Linguistics (EACL-2006)*, Trento, Italy.

G. Katz and E. Giesbrecht. 2006. Automatic identification of non-compositional multi-word expressions using Latent Semantic Analysis. In *Proc. of the COLING/ACL'06 Workshop on Multiword Expressions: Identifying and Exploiting Underlying Properties*, pages 12–19, Sydney, Australia.

D. Lin. 1998. Automatic retrieval and clustering of similar words. In *Proceedings of* COLING/ACL *98*, Montreal, Canada.

D. Lin. 1999. Automatic identification of non-compositional phrases. In *Proceedings of ACL-99*, pages 317–324. University of Maryland.

J. B. MacQueen. 1967. Some methods for classification and analysis of multivariate observations. In *Proceedings of 5-th Berkeley Symposium on Mathematical Statistics and Probability*, volume 1, pages 281–297, Berkeley. University of California Press.

W. Martin and I. Maks, 2005. *Referentie Bestand Nederlands. Documentatie*, April.

D. McCarthy, B. Keller, and J. Carroll. 2003. Detecting a Continuum of Compositionality in Phrasal Verbs. In *Proc. of the ACL-2003 Workshop on Multiword Expressions: Analysis, Acquisition and Treatment*, Sapporo, Japan.

R.J.F. Ordelman. 2002. Twente Nieuws Corpus (TwNC), August. Parlevink Language Techonology Group. University of Twente.

D. Pearce. 2001. Synonymy in collocation extraction. In *WordNet and Other lexical resources: applications, extensions & customizations (NAACL 2001)*, pages 41–46, Pittsburgh. Carnegie Mellon University.

S. Piao, P. Rayson, O. Mudraya, A. Wilson, and R. Garside. 2006. Measuring mwe compositionality using semantic annotation. In *Proceedings of the Workshop on Multiword Expressions: Identifying and Exploiting Underlying Properties*, pages 2–11, Sydney, Australia. Association for Computational Linguistics.

P. Resnik. 1993. *Selection and Information: A Class-Based Approach to Lexical Relationships*. PhD Thesis, University of Pennsylvania.

P. Resnik. 1996. Selectional constraints: An information-theoretic model and its computational realization. *Cognition*, 61:127–159.

I. Sag, T. Baldwin, F. Bond, A. Copestake, and D. Flickinger. 2002. Multiword Expressions: a pain in the neck for NLP. In *Proceedings of the Third International Conference on Intelligent Text Processing and Computational Linguistics*, pages 1–15, Mexico City, Mexico.

L. van der Plas and G. Bouma. 2005. Syntactic contexts for finding semantically similar words. *Computational Linguistics in the Netherlands 2004. Selected Papers from the Fifteenth CLIN Meeting*, pages 173–184.

G. van Noord. 2006. At Last Parsing Is Now Operational. In P. Mertens, C. Fairon, A. Dister, and P. Watrin, editors, *TALN06. Verbum Ex Machina. Actes de la 13e conference sur le traitement automatique des langues naturelles*, pages 20–42, Leuven.

S. Venkatapathy and A. Joshi. 2005. Measuring the relative compositionality of verb-noun collocations by integrating features. In *Proceedings of the Human Language Technology Conference and Conference on Empirical Methods in Natural Language Processing*, pages 899–906, Vancouver.

B. Villada Moirón and J. Tiedemann. 2006. Identifying idiomatic expressions using automatic word-alignment. In *Proceedings of the EACL 2006 Workshop on Multi-word-expressions in a multilingual context"*, pages 33–40, Trento, Italy.

J. Weeds. 2003. *Measures and Applications of Lexical Distributional Similarity*. PhD Thesis, University of Sussex.

Z. Wu and M. Palmer. 1994. Verb semantics and lexical selection. In *32nd. Annual Meeting of the Association for Computational Linguistics*, pages 133–138, New Mexico State University, Las Cruces, New Mexico.

Spanish Adverbial Frozen Expressions

Dolors Català
Autonomous University of Barcelona
Campus Sabadell, 08202, Spain
*f*LexSem
dolors.catala@uab.cat

Jorge Baptista
Univ.Algarve, Campus de Gambelas
P-8005-139 Faro, Portugal
L[2]F – INESC-ID Lisboa, Portugal
jbaptis@ualg.pt

Abstract

This paper presents an electronic dictionary of Spanish adverbial frozen expressions. It focuses on their formal description in view of natural language processing and presents an experiment on the automatic application of this data to real texts using finite-state techniques. The paper makes an assessment of the advantages and limitations of this method for the identification of these multiword units in texts.

1 Introduction

We have undertaken the construction of an electronic dictionary of compound adverbs, or adverbial frozen expressions (Català 2003). This dictionary completes the DELACs, i.e., the dictionary of compound words of Spanish (Blanco and Català (1998)).

These adverbial frozen expressions (*a tontas y a locas = by fits and starts, como anillo al dedo = like a glove; a ojo de buen cubero = at a guess*)[1] have often been considered as exceptions but they constitute an important part of the lexicon.

Their formal description highlights many problems for NLP applications. On the one hand, they are multiword expressions functioning as meaning units, so they have to be recognized as a block and are not to be analyzed as a free sequence of simple words. On the other hand, they present, sometimes, some lexical variation that can take complex lexical syntactical patterns.

[1] Approximate translations of examples do not intend to be fully acceptable, but to illustrate syntactic phenomena.

For example, some adverbs show combinatorial constraints between discontinuous elements:

*día sí, día no / año si, año no,*día si, año no*
'on even days/years'.

Others yet present long distance dependencies:

[***Yo*** *estudio*] *con todas* **mis/*sus** *fuerzas*
'(I study) with all my/his strength');

Lexical variation of the compound elements is often constraint in an unpredictable way:

[*Juan aprobó*] *por los/*todos los/*sus/*unos pelos*
'(John passed the exam) with difficulties'

Some allow for a theoretically infinite paradigm as in the expression <Card> *veces seguidas* '<number> of times in a row', where *Card* stands for a numeral, whose meaning is compositional but whose form is fixed:

[*Eso sucedió*] *Card veces seguidas*
'(It happened) <number> of times in a row'

since the adjective does not allow for any variation:

*[*Eso sucedió*] *Card veces continuas*
'(It happened) <number> of times in a row'

In some cases, the adjective can not be reduced:

[*Juan dijo esto*] *en voz baja / *en voz*
'(John said this) in low voice/in voice'

nor can it be placed before the noun:

[*Juan dijo esto*] *en voz baja / *en baja voz*
'(John said this) in voice low /in low voice'

2 The Dictionary

The theoretical and methodological framework adopted is the lexicon-grammar based on the principles of the transformational grammar of Harris (1976, 1997) developed by Maurice Gross

Proceedings of the Workshop on A Broader Perspective on Multiword Expressions, pages 33–40,
Prague, June 2007. ©2007 Association for Computational Linguistics

(1986). In this perspective, the adverbial frozen expressions are formalized in the frame of simple sentences and their network of paraphrastic relations. Adverbs are predicates that necessarily apply on other predicates and have a basic influence in their selection. For example, some adverbs are only associated with a limited number of verbs[2]:

[*Juan duerme/pernocta/pasa la noche*] *al raso*
'(John sleeps) in the open air'

While some others are only used in a negative sentence:

[*Juan* ***no*** *aceptará*] *por nada del mundo*
'(John will not accept) by no means'

*[*Juan aceptará*] *por nada del mundo*
'(John will accept) by no means'

Others impose a specific tense:

[*Juan* ***llegará***] *en breve* '(John *will* come shortly'

*[*John llegó*] *en breve* '(John has come) shortly'

2.1 Classification

We apply the notion of adverbs to syntactically different structures of traditional terminology such as underived (primary) adverbs (*bien*, 'well') or derived forms (*profundamente* 'deeply'), circumstantial complements (*al amanecer* 'at dawn'), and circumstantial clauses (*hasta que la muerte nos separe* 'until death do us part').

We considered the sequence *Prep Det C Modif*[3] as the basic structure that formally define and classify compound adverbs, adopting the concept of *generalized adverb* proposed by M. Gross (1986) for French adverbs.

Based on this, we defined 15 formal classes for Spanish compound adverbs. Table 1 (below) shows the current state of the dictionary, the internal structure of each class, an illustrative example and the number of compound adverbs collected so far.

Further than this classification based on their internal structure, we have proposed different types of semantic-functional groups presented in terms of Finite State Transducers (FSTs), as in Fig.1. In this graph, all adverbial expressions have the same general meaning ('quickly'). Similar graphs can be used, for example, to compare the distribution of semantically 'equivalent' expressions and to structure the co-occurrence of those adverbs with their argument predicates.

Class	Structure	Example	Size
PC	*Prep C*	*sin ambajes*	869
PDETC	*Prep Det C*	*al contado*	585
PAC	*Prep Adj C*	*sin previo aviso*	157
PCA	*Prep C Adj*	*a brazo partido*	291
PCDC	*Prep C de C*	*a cuerpo de rey*	168
PCPC	*Prep C Prep C*	*de cabo a rabo*	149
PCONJ	*Prep C Conj C*	*en cuerpo y alma*	131
PCDN	*Prep C de N*	*a condición de*	233
PCPN	*Prep C Prep N*	*de espaldas a*	51
PV	*Prep V W*	*sin querer*	127
PF	frozen sentence	*que yo sepa*	169
PECO	*(como) Adj que C*	*sordo como una tapia*	797
PVCO	*(V) como C*	*(beber) como una esponja*	532
PPCO	*(V) como Prep C*	*(desaparecer) como por ensalmo*	46
PJC	*Conj C*	*y no se hable más*	91
		TOTAL	4396

Table 1. Classification of Spanish compound adverbs

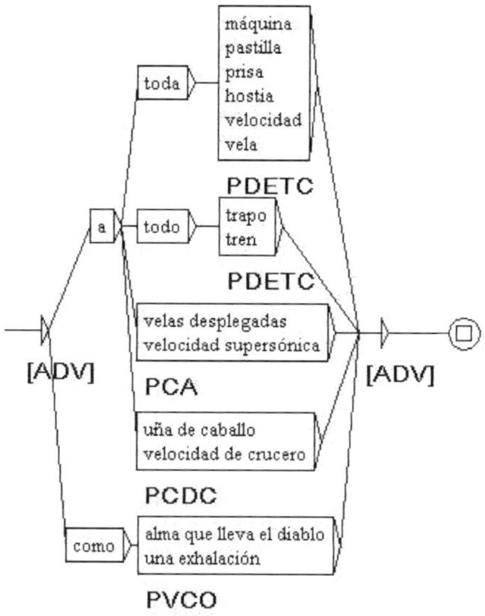

Fig.1 Finite-State graph (simplified) for semantic clustering of adverbs

2.2 Microstructure of Dictionary

The description takes the shape of binary matrices (see Table 2, for an example), in which each line corresponds to a lexical entry, and the columns represent different information. The set of matrices constitute the lexicon-grammar of adverbial frozen expressions. Next, we present a brief description of the microstructure of the dictionary.

[2] In the examples, (argument) simple sentences are given in brackets.

[3] *Prep* = preposition; *Det* = determiner; *C* = lexical constant, usually a noun; *Modif* = modifier, such as an adjective (*Adj*) or a prepositional phrase.

N_0	V	Prep	Det	C	PreMod	Mod	Prép Dét C	Prép Dét Adj C	Conj	DiaSys	English equivalent
hum	Vact	-	-	acto	-	seguido	-	-	+	-	immediately afterwards
hum	llegar	a	la	hora	-	horada	+	-	-	familiar	on the nose
hum	Vact	por	-	voluntad	-	propia	-	+	-	-	with one's own will
hum	comprar	a	el	por	-	mayor	-	-	-	commerce	wholesale
hum	dormir	con	los	ojos	medio	abiertos	-	-	-	-	with one's eyes half open

Table 2. Class PCA (extract)

The first column concerns the syntactic-semantic nature of the subject. We adopted G. Gross (1995) and Le Pesant and Mathieu-Colas (1989) basic typology, distinguishing the following semantic classes: *human, animal, vegetal, concrete,* and *abstract*.

The second column refers to the verb most commonly used with the adverb, for example:

[*salir*] *a cuerpo gentil*
'(to go out) without cloak';

[*cerrar Nconc*] *a cal y canto*
'(to close something) under lock and key'.

The following columns contain the elements of the structure: *Prep, Det, C,* and *Modif*, e.g.:

[*Esta gente llegó en este país*] *con las manos vacías*
'These people arrived in this country with empty hands'

Naturally, in Spanish the modifier can be placed before *C*:

[Se peleaban] *a la menor ocasión*
'(they were fighting each others) at the least occasion/opportunity'.

The next columns correspond to their syntactic (distributional and transformational) properties: '+' indicates that the expression admits this property, and '- ' that it does not. Relevant properties depend on the class: some have to do with permutation of elements of the compound or their reduction to zero (zeroing); see §2.3, below.

Diasystem information (Hausmann 1989) is provided in next field (DiaSys) such as these categories (marked in bold, in the examples below):

- diatopy:
  [*Juan trabaja*] *al cohete* (Uruguay/Argentina)
  '(John works) in vain';
- diachrony :
  [*Juan convoca a los estudiantes*] *a voz de apellido* (**out of use**)
  '(John summons the students) by their family name';
- diafrequency :
  [*Juan se sirvió*] *a barba regada* (**unusual**)
  '(John served himself) abundantly'
- diastratic:
  [*Juan recita*] *de carretilla* (**familiar/ colloquial**)
  '(John recites) by heart';
- diatechnical :
  [*El torero clavó la banderilla*] *de sobaquillo* (**bullfighting**) '(the bull fighter has pinched the bull) on its side;
- diaintegrative :
  [*Juan vino*] *motu propio* (**latinism**)
  '(John came) voluntarily'.

Finally, we have included French translation equivalents. These equivalence relations are also currently being extended to other languages, such as Portuguese (Palma, *in prep.*).

2.3 Syntactic properties

We will only consider here the most prominent properties, considering all classes of adverbs under study.

One of the properties indicates the possibility to transform the initial structure in to a more analytical phrase like *de (modo + manera) C-a* 'in a *C-a* way/manner', where *C-a* is an adjective, morphologically related to the constant (frozen element) *C*; naturally the meaning of the two structures is the same:

[*La candidatura se aprobó*] *por unanimidad*
= [*La candidatura se aprobó*] *de manera unánime*

'(His application was approved) by unanimity/in an unanimous way'

[Juan lo ha dicho] con todos los respetos
= *[Juan lo ha dicho] de manera respetuosa*
'(John has said so) with all due respect/ in a respectful manner'.

Another, similar, property shows the possibility to transform the initial structure in an adverb based on the same type of *C-a* adjective and the suffix *-mente.* This property concerns classes PC and PDETC :

[La candidatura se aprobó] por unanimidad
= *[La candidatura se aprobó] unánimemente*
'(His application was approved) unanimously'

[Juan lo ha dicho] con todos los respetos
= *[Juan lo ha dicho] respetuosamente*
'(John has said so) respectfully'.

Property *Conj* concerns classes PC, PDETC, PAC and PCA. It highlights the eventual anaphoric effect of the adverb. We consider it as a conjunction-adverb, since in sentences like:

[Juan estudia] en consecuencia
'(John studies) in consequence'

[Juan se marchó] por lo tanto
'(John went away) for that much'

we need a (trans-)phrastic context such as :

[Juan quiere aprobar], en consecuencia, [estudia].
'(John wants to succeed in school), in consequence (he studies)'

[Ana se enfadó con Juan], por lo tanto, [éste se marchó]
'(Ana get bored with John), for that much (he went away)'

The next property concerns classes PCA and PAC. It describes the possible omission of the modifier:

[Los niños andan] en fila india
'(The kids walk) in Indian line'
= *[los niños andan] en fila*
'(The kids walk) in line'

Other property indicates the possibility of moving modifier from its basic position to the left of *C*; it only concerns class PCA:

[Juan encontró a Ana] en hora buena
= *[Juan encontró a Ana] en buena hora*
'(John met Ana) in good time/in time'

We have also noted the possibility of zeroing the second element of the compound, i.e., the free or frozen prepositional phrase. It concerns classes PCDC, PCPC, PCONJ, PCPN, and PCDN:

[Juan estudia] con la mejor voluntad del mundo
= *[Juan estudia] con la mejor voluntad*
'(John studies) with the best will (of the world)'

[Juan vive] al margen de la sociedad
= *[Juan vive] al margen*
'(John lives) at the margin (of society)'

[Juan vive] de espaldas a la calle
= *[Juan vive] de espaldas*
'(John lives) with his back (turned to the street)'

Certain permutations have been noted, but not dealt with in a transformational way:

[Juan se enamoró de Ana] por decirlo así
= *[Juan se enamoró de Ana] por así decirlo*
'(John fall in love with Ana) as it were'

Finally, we consider the possibility of substitution of the second element by a subordinate clause (finite or infinitive); this property concerns PCDN and PCPN:

[Le consultará] en caso de duda
= *[Le consultará] en caso de que haya duda*
'(He will consult him) in case of doubt/in case there is any doubt'

[Juan se marchó] por miedo al fuego
= *[Juan se marchó] por miedo a que haya fuego*
'(He went away) for fear of fire/there being fire'

[Juan se sujetó] por miedo a una caída
'(John hold tight) by fear of a fall'
= *[Juan se sujetó] por miedo a caer*
'(John hold tight) by fear of to fall'

A strictly statistically, corpus-based approach that only contemplates strings of words in view to produce lexicon entries (Manning and Schütze 2003) cannot but fail to put in relation such formal variants of equivalent expressions. On the other hand, many formal variations are very much dependent on the particular lexical combinations, and cannot be generalized, hence the need to describe their syntactic properties systematically.

While very time-consuming, our method provides a fine-grained linguistic description, and is directly exploitable by finite-state methods.

With the aim of retrieving the adverbial expressions from texts using the information encoded in the lexicon matrices, it should be noted that most but not all properties referred to above can be directly formalized using the finite-state methods we are currently using. In the following lines, we present this methodology.

3 Formalization

In order to apply to texts the set of matrices that constitute the Lexicon-Grammar and thus to identify and tag compound adverbs, we have followed the methodology proposed by Senellart (1998) and Silberztein (2000), and adapted by Paumier (2003, 2004) for the UNITEX system [4]. This method consists of intersecting linguistic data on matrices with a finite-state graph (called a reference graph) in order to generate automatically a finite-state transducer (FST) that can be applied to a corpus[5].

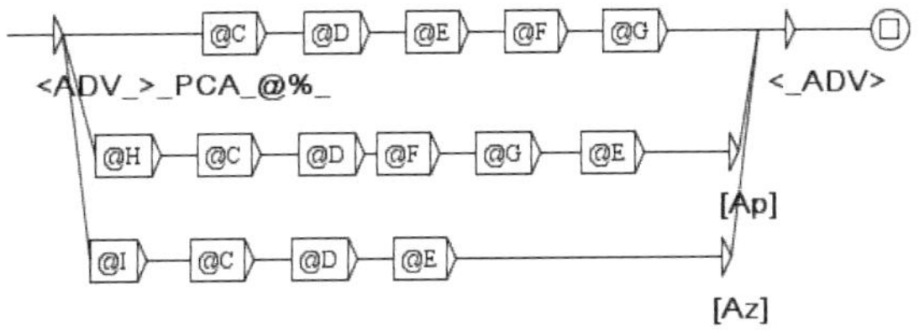

Fig.2 Reference graph (simplified) for class PCA

Fig.2 shows a (simplified) reference graph for class PCA. In the graph, variable @X stands for column X in the matrix. For each line in the matrix the system builds a sub-graph by replacing each variable for the content of the corresponding columns in the matrix. If that columns is a binary property, the corresponding variable in the graph functions as a switch, allowing for the rest of that graph's path to be build in case of a '+' or, else, collapsing the graph at that point, if a '-' is found at that property. It is also possible to deny a property (!@X), which has the opposite effect. Another utility of the system is the inclusion of a variable @% that outputs the number of each entry line in the matrix, thus enabling the user to easily put in correspondence a given result to the corresponding lexical entry. The set of sub-graphs (one per each entry in the matrix) is automatically gathered in a finite-state transducer that can be directly applied to texts.

In Fig. 2, class PCA reference graph includes: two delimiters of the compound expression, <ADV_> and <_ADV> ; the @% variable; the top-most path describe the full expression, while the second and third paths, below, depend on properties described by variables @H and @I; these correspond to the permutation of the adjective [Ap] and its reduction to zero [Az], respectively.

Similar graphs have been built to other classes[6]. The set of classes thus formalized constitute an electronic dictionary of 2,930 entries (67% of all compound entries collected so far).

4 An experiment on texts

The aim of this experiment is to assess the advantages and limitations of the methodology described in §3 in the identification of multiword units, in this case, compound adverbs, in real texts in Spanish.

The FSTs were applied to a fragment of a corpus of journalistic text taken from the newspaper *El Mundo*, of about 2 Mb and 171.5 K (~24 K different) words. The system retrieved 2,276 matches, corresponding to 461 different entries.

Table 3 shows the breakdown of these matches per class and its percentage, followed by the number of different entries (types) matched by the system and the corresponding percentage of each class entries.

class	class size	matches	% matches	entrie s	% entries
PC	869	849	0.37	215	0,47
PCDN	233	489	0.22	12	0,03
PDETC	585	406	0.18	119	0,26
PCPN	51	238	0.10	23	0,05
PCA	291	134	0.06	19	0,04
PF	169	42	0.02	7	0,02
PAC	157	38	0.02	23	0,05
PCONJ	131	22	0.01	9	0,02
PCPC	149	21	0.01	12	0,03
PCDC	168	17	0.01	12	0,03
PV	127	16	0.01	10	0,02
	2,930	2,272		461	

Table 3. Breakdown of matches per class.

Classes PC, PCDN, PDETC, PCPN and PCA are the only classes with over 100 matches; together they constitute 93% of the matches, all other classes have residual expression.

[4] www.univ-mlv.fr/~unitex.

[5] See Paumier (2004), for further details.

[6] In this paper, however, we did not deal with classes of comparative adverbs (PECO, PVCO and PPCO) or class PJC, which pose particular problems to their recognition.

On the other hand, classes PC and PDETC present the larger number of dictionary entries matched. Notice that, despite the number of entries in the matrices, only 461 entries (16%) were found in the corpus.

Class PC alone represents 47% of the total entries matched by the system (215/461), immediately followed by class PDETC, with 26% of matched entries (119/461). Matches for these two classes together constitute 55% of the total of strings matched by the system (1,255/2,272). These two figures make PC and PDETC the most prominent classes for this experiment, in view of the assessment of the finite-state methods here used to identify compound adverbs in texts. For lack of space, analysis of results will thus focus on these classes and only major phenomena, i.e., those situations with major impact on results, will be taken in consideration here.

5 Results and discussion

We went through the concordances manually, and confirmed a **precision** of 77.4% (974/1,255) [7]. We discuss these results below.

The major reason for incorrect matching has been found to correspond to cases where the matched sequence is not the target compound adverb but part of a longer, free word sequence, or part of a compound word; in the following example, the adverb *de accidente* 'accidentally' is an ambiguous string since it overlaps with the compound noun *seguros de accidente* 'accident insurances'

Antes de iniciar un rodaje, se prevé cualquier eventualidad. Se contratan **seguros *de accidente*,** *enfermedad y muerte para las personas clave del proyecto* [PC_0010]

while in the next example, the string *de derecho* 'by law/right' overlaps a (free) prepositional phrase which includes a compound noun *derecho de veto* 'right of veto':

Yo creo que no se puede pretender ejercer una especie ***de derecho*** **de veto**, *porque esto querría decir que el Gobierno es rehén* [PC_0243]

In some few cases, incorrect matches were the result of an inadequate treatment of contractions of prepositions and determiners. In classes PCDN, PCPN, the second preposition often appears contracted with the determiner of the free NP. In the next example, contraction of *a* + *el* = *al* has not been correctly described:

coches serán introducidos en el mercado nipón en el mes de octubre, con ocasión del Salón de Tokio. ***Con respecto*** **al Tigra**, *que se produce en exclusiva para todo el mundo en Figuer* [PC_0686]

This problem is to be fixed on a next version of the reference FSTs.

In some cases, especially when the adverb is marked as a conjunction-adverb (*Conj*), it often appears between comas or at the beginning of sentences, followed by coma.

se había montado su particular Guerra de los Mundos de tema ferroviario. También hay quien piensa, ***por cierto,*** *que a este Gobierno se lo van a cargar no sus errores, sino las cos* [PC_0145]

privatizar el 99,9% de las empresas y entes públicos de la Comunidad y ya está trabajando en ello. ***Por cierto,*** *le ha arrebatado el control del Canal de Isabel II a Pedroche y lo* [PC_0145]

We have annotated these cases so that this information can be added to the matrices and used in disambiguation tasks.

Finally, many temporal adverbs have only partially been identified.

puede seguir así»- exigió al Gobierno de González que fije un calendario electoral **antes del 17 de *este mes*.** *Tras de lo cual, el aún secretario general de CDC sostuvo que, si* [PDETC_0076]

zo de Erez, consiguió dos objetivos. En primer lugar, Israel se comprometió a iniciar, **a finales de *este mes*,** *la evacuación gradual de tres ciudades palestinas: Jenin, Kalkilia* [PDETC_0076]

This occurs because matrices only included simple word combinations. As others have noted previously (Baptista and Català 2002; Baptista 2003a,b), time-related adverbs may be described by FST methods as those used here. Those local grammars could easily be integrated in the system.

[7] Since we started with a previously, manually build, electronic dictionary, we can not compute *recall*. We define *precision* as the number of correct matches on total matches.

6 Conclusion

The taxonomic approach adopted here, the systematic survey of the lexicon and its formal representation, resulted in a complex linguistic database of Spanish compound adverbs. This may have many applications, not strictly in Linguistics, but also in Didactics and in Lexicography.

It can further be used in several applications on natural language processing. The relatively high precision (77,4%) of the finite state methods used in this paper are very encouraging, and in some cases, discussed above, they can and will be improved in a future version both of the reference graphs and of the lexicon-grammar matrices.

However, the major difficulty to a better identification of compound adverbs in texts seems to reside in the fact that no syntactic analysis (parsing) has been performed on the text. Therefore, there is no possibility of using information regarding (sub-)phrases and other constituents of the compounds in order to preclude incorrect matching.

Another aspect that hinders better results has to do with the formal variation of compound adverbial expressions. Adverbs present more problems for their recognition as the limit between free sequence and fixed sequence is more difficult to establish than in others categories of compounds. The building of electronic dictionaries may benefit from a (more) corpus-based approach, so as to retrieve variants of a given lexical entry, but a careful and time-consuming verification is needed in order to group variants as different expressions of the same meaning unit.

Finally, the relatively small portion of the dictionary matched on the corpus imposes that it should be tested on texts of a more diverse nature and of a larger size, thus probably yielding a larger perspective of the use of these idiomatic expressions. Still, it is now possible to consider the study of the distribution of these adverbs, trying to specify the type of predicates (verbs, nouns, adjectives, mainly) on which they operate.

Acknowledgement

This research was supported by the Spanish Ministerio de Ciencia y Tecnologia in the framework of the project grant HP-2004-0098, and Conselho de Reitores das Universidades Portuguesas, project grant E-111/-05.

References

Jorge Baptista 2003a. Some Families of Compound Temporal Adverbs in Portuguese. Proceedings of Workshop on *Finite-State Methods for Natural Language Processing*: 97-104, ACL, Hungary.

Jorge Baptista 2003b. Evaluation of Finite-State Lexical Transducers of Temporal Adverbs for Lexical Analysis of Portuguese Texts. *Computational Processing of the Portuguese Language.* Proceedings of *PROPOR'2003.* Lecture Notes in Computer Science/Lecture Notes in Artificial Intelligence 2721: 235-242, Springer, Berlin.

Jorge Baptista and Dolors Català 2002. Compound Temporal Adverbs in Portuguese and in Spanish. *Advances in Natural Language Processing*, Lecture Notes in Computer Science/Lecture Notes in Artificial Intelligence 2389: 133-136, Springer, Berlin.

Jorge Baptista and Dolors Català 2006. Les adverbes composés dans le domaine du travail. *Mots, Termes, et Contextes*: 249-263, AUF/LTT and Éd. Archives Contemporaines, Paris.

Xavier Blanco and Dolors Català 1998. Quelques remarques sur un dictionnaire électronique d'adverbes composés en espagnol. *Linguisticae Investigationes Supplementa* 11 (2): 213-232, John Benjamins Pub. Co., Amsterdam/Philadelphia.

Gaston Gross 1995. À propos de la notion d'humain. *Lexiques Grammaires Comparés en Français. inguisticae Investigationes Supplementa* 17: 71-80, John Benjamins Pub. Co., Amsterdam/Philadelphia.

Maurice Gross 1986. *Grammaire transformationnelle du français: syntaxe de l'adverbe,* ASSTRIL, Paris.

Zellig S. Harris 1976 *Notes du cours de syntaxe,* Le Seuil, Paris.

Zellig S. Harris. *A Theory of Language and Information. A Mathematical Approach*, Clarendon Press, Oxford.

Franz J. Haussmann 1989. Die Markierung in allgemeinen einsprachigen Wörterbuch: eine Übersicht, *Wörterbücher, Dictionaries, Dictionnaires*, vol 1: 651, Berlin/ New York, Walter de Gruyter.

Denis Le Pesant and Michel Mathieu-Colas. 1998. Introduction aux classes d'objets *Langages* 131: 6-33, Larousse, Paris.

Ch. Manning and H. Schütze 2003. *Foundations of Statistical Natural Language Processing*, MIT Press, London/Cambridge, MA

Cristina Palma (in preparation). *Estudo Contrastivo Português-Espanhol de Advérbios Compostos*, Univ. Algarve, Faro.

Sébastien Paumier 2004. *Unitex - manuel d'utilisation*, Univ. Marne-la-Vallée, Paris.

Jean Senellart 1998. Reconnaissance automatique des entrées du lexique-grammaire des phrases figées. *Le Lexique-Grammaire. Travaux de Linguistique* 37: 109-125, Duculot, Bruxelles.

Max Silberztein 2000. *Intex* (Manual), ASSTRIL/LADL, Paris.

Pulling their Weight: Exploiting Syntactic Forms for the Automatic Identification of Idiomatic Expressions in Context

Paul Cook and Afsaneh Fazly and Suzanne Stevenson
Department of Computer Science
University of Toronto
Toronto, Canada
{pcook,afsaneh,suzanne}@cs.toronto.edu

Abstract

Much work on idioms has focused on type identification, i.e., determining whether a sequence of words can form an idiomatic expression. Since an idiom type often has a literal interpretation as well, token classification of potential idioms in context is critical for NLP. We explore the use of informative prior knowledge about the overall syntactic behaviour of a potentially-idiomatic expression (type-based knowledge) to determine whether an instance of the expression is used idiomatically or literally (token-based knowledge). We develop unsupervised methods for the task, and show that their performance is comparable to that of state-of-the-art supervised techniques.

1 Introduction

Identification of multiword expressions (MWEs), such as *car park*, *make a decision*, and *kick the bucket*, is extremely important for accurate natural language processing (NLP) (Sag et al., 2002). Most MWEs need to be treated as single units of meaning, e.g., *make a decision* roughly means "decide". Nonetheless, the components of an MWE can be separated, making it hard for an NLP system to identify the expression as a whole. Many researchers have recently developed methods for the automatic acquisition of various properties of MWEs from corpora (Lin, 1999; Krenn and Evert, 2001; Baldwin et al., 2003; McCarthy et al., 2003; Venkatapathy and Joshi, 2005; Villada Moirón and Tiedemann, 2006; Fazly and Stevenson, 2006). These studies look into properties, such as the collocational behaviour of MWEs, their semantic non-compositionality, and their lexicosyntactic fixedness, in order to distinguish them from similar-on-the-surface literal combinations.

Most of these methods have been aimed at recognizing MWE types; less attention has been paid to the identification of instances (tokens) of MWEs in context. For example, most such techniques (if successful) would identify *make a face* as a potential MWE. This expression is, however, ambiguous between an idiom, as in *The little girl made a funny face at her mother*, and a literal combination, as in *She made a face on the snowman using a carrot and two buttons*. Despite the common perception that phrases that can be idioms are mainly used in their idiomatic sense, our analysis of 60 idioms has shown otherwise. We found that close to half of these idioms also have a clear literal meaning; and of the expressions with a literal meaning, on average around 40% of their usages are literal. Distinguishing token phrases as MWEs or literal combinations of words is thus essential for NLP applications that require the identification of multiword semantic units, such as semantic parsing and machine translation.

Recent studies addressing MWE token classification mainly perform the task as one of word sense disambiguation, and draw on the local context of an expression to disambiguate it. Such techniques either do not use any information regarding the linguistic properties of MWEs (Birke and Sarkar, 2006), or mainly focus on their non-compositionality (Katz and Giesbrecht, 2006). Pre-

Proceedings of the Workshop on A Broader Perspective on Multiword Expressions, pages 41–48,
Prague, June 2007. ©2007 Association for Computational Linguistics

vious work on the identification of MWE types, however, has found other properties of MWEs, such as their syntactic fixedness, to be relevant to their identification (Evert et al., 2004; Fazly and Stevenson, 2006). In this paper, we propose techniques that draw on this property to classify individual tokens of a potentially idiomatic phrase as literal or idiomatic. We also put forward classification techniques that combine such information with evidence from the local context of an MWE.

We explore the hypothesis that informative prior knowledge about the overall syntactic behaviour of an idiomatic expression (type-based knowledge) can be used to determine whether an instance of the expression is used literally or idiomatically (token-based knowledge). Based on this hypothesis, we develop unsupervised methods for token classification, and show that their performance is comparable to that of a standard supervised method.

Many verbs can be combined with one or more of their arguments to form MWEs (Cowie et al., 1983; Fellbaum, 2002). Here, we focus on a broadly documented class of idiomatic MWEs that are formed from the combination of a verb with a noun in its direct object position, as in *make a face*. In the rest of the paper, we refer to these verb+noun combinations, which are potentially idiomatic, as VNCs. In Section 2, we propose unsupervised methods that classify a VNC token as an idiomatic or literal usage. Section 3 describes our experimental setup, including experimental expressions and their annotation. In Section 4, we present a detailed discussion of our results. Section 5 compares our work with similar previous studies, and Section 6 concludes the paper.

2 Unsupervised Idiom Identification

We first explain an important linguistic property attributed to idioms—that is, their syntactic fixedness (Section 2.1). We then propose unsupervised methods that draw on this property to automatically distinguish between idiomatic and literal usages of an expression (Section 2.2).

2.1 Syntactic Fixedness and Canonical Forms

Idioms tend to be somewhat fixed with respect to the syntactic configurations in which they occur (Nunberg et al., 1994). For example, *pull one's weight* tends to mainly appear in this form when used idiomatically. Other forms of the expression, such as *pull the weights*, typically are only used with a literal meaning. In their work on automatically identifying idiom types, Fazly and Stevenson (2006)—henceforth FS06—show that an idiomatic VNC tends to have one (or at most a small number of) canonical form(s), which are its most preferred syntactic patterns. The preferred patterns can vary across different idiom types, and can involve a number of syntactic properties: the voice of the verb (active or passive), the determiner introducing the noun (*the*, *one's*, etc.), and the number of the noun (singular or plural). For example, while *pull one's weight* has only one canonical form, *hold fire* and *hold one's fire* are two canonical forms of the same idiom, as listed in an idiom dictionary (Seaton and Macaulay, 2002).

In our work, we assume that in most cases, idiomatic usages of an expression tend to occur in a small number of canonical form(s) for that idiom. We also assume that, in contrast, the literal usages of an expression are less syntactically restricted, and are expressed in a greater variety of patterns. Because of their relative unrestrictiveness, literal usages may occur in a canonical idiomatic form for that expression, but usages in a canonical form are more likely to be idiomatic. Usages in alternative syntactic patterns for the expression, which we refer to as the non-canonical forms of the idiom, are more likely to be literal. Drawing on these assumptions, we develop three unsupervised methods that determine, for each VNC token in context, whether it has an idiomatic or a literal interpretation.

2.2 Statistical Methods

The following paragraphs elaborate on our proposed methods for identifying the idiomatic and literal usages of a VNC: the CForm method that uses knowledge of canonical forms only, and two Diff methods that draw on further contextual evidence as well. All three methods draw on our assumptions described above, that usages in the canonical form for an idiom are more likely to be idiomatic, and those in other forms are more likely to be literal. Thus, for all three methods, we need access to the canonical form of the idiom. Since we want our token identification methods to be unsupervised, we adopt the unsupervised statistical method of FS06 for finding canonical forms for an idiomatic VNC. This method determines the canonical forms of an expression to be those forms whose frequency is much higher than the average frequency of all its forms.

CForm: The underlying assumption of this method is that information about the canonical form(s) of an idiom type is extremely informative in classifying the meaning of its individual instances (tokens) as literal or idiomatic. Our CForm classifies a token as idiomatic if it occurs in the automatically determined canonical form(s) for that expression, and as literal otherwise.

Diff: Our two Diff methods combine local context information with knowledge about the canonical forms of an idiom type to determine if its token usages are literal or idiomatic. In developing these methods, we adopt a distributional approach to meaning, where the meaning of an expression is approximated by the words with which it co-occurs (Firth, 1957). Although there may be fine-grained differences in meaning across the idiomatic usages of an expression, as well as across its literal usages, we assume that the idiomatic and literal usages correspond to two coarse-grained senses of the expression. Since we further assume these two groups of usages will have more in common semantically within each group than between the two groups, we expect that literal and idiomatic usages of an expression will typically occur with different sets of words. We will refer then to each of the literal and idiomatic designations as a (coarse-grained) meaning of the expression, while acknowledging that each may have multiple fine-grained senses. Clearly, the success of our method depends on the extent to which these assumptions hold.

We estimate the meaning of a set of usages of an expression e as a word frequency vector $\vec{v}_e$ where each dimension i of $\vec{v}_e$ is the frequency with which e co-occurs with word i across the usages of e. We similarly estimate the meaning of a single token of an expression t as a vector $\vec{v}_t$ capturing that usage. To determine if an instance of an expression is literal or idiomatic, we compare its co-occurrence vector to the co-occurrence vectors representing each of the literal and idiomatic meanings of the expression. We use a standard measure of distributional similarity, cosine, to compare co-occurrence vectors.

In supervised approaches, such as that of Katz and Giesbrecht (2006), co-occurrence vectors for literal and idiomatic meanings are formed from manually-annotated training data. Here, we propose unsupervised methods for estimating these vectors. We use one way of estimating the idiomatic meaning of an expression, and two ways for estimating its literal meaning, yielding two methods for token classification.

Our first Diff method draws further on our expectation that canonical forms are more likely idiomatic usages, and non-canonical forms are more likely literal usages. We estimate the idiomatic meaning of an expression by building a co-occurrence vector, $\vec{v}_{I\text{-}CF}$, for all uses of the expression in its automatically determined canonical form(s). Since we hypothesize that idiomatic usages of an expression tend to occur in its canonical form, we expect these co-occurrence vectors to be largely representative of the idiomatic usage of the expression. We similarly estimate the literal meaning by constructing a co-occurrence vector, $\vec{v}_{L\text{-}NCF}$, of all uses of the expression in its non-canonical forms. We use the term $\text{Diff}_{I\text{-}CF,L\text{-}NCF}$ to refer to this method.

Our second Diff method also uses the vector $\vec{v}_{I\text{-}CF}$ to estimate the idiomatic meaning of an expression. However, this approach follows that of Katz and Giesbrecht (2006) in assuming that literal meanings are compositional. The literal meaning of an expression is thus estimated by composing (summing and then normalizing) the co-occurrence vectors for its component words. The resulting vector is referred to as $\vec{v}_{L\text{-}Comp}$, and this method as $\text{Diff}_{I\text{-}CF,L\text{-}Comp}$.

For both Diff methods, if the meaning of an instance of an expression is determined to be more similar to its idiomatic meaning (e.g., $\text{cosine}(\vec{v}_t, \vec{v}_{I\text{-}CF}) > \text{cosine}(\vec{v}_t, \vec{v}_{L\text{-}NCF})$), then we label it as an idiomatic usage. Otherwise, it is labeled as literal.[1]

[1]We also performed experiments using a KNN classifier in which the co-occurrence vector for a token was compared against the co-occurrence vectors for the canonical and non-canonical forms of that expression, which were assumed to be idiomatic and literal usages respectively. However, performance was generally worse using this method.

Note that all three of our proposed techniques for token identification depend on how accurately the canonical forms of an expression can be acquired. FS06's canonical form acquisition technique, which we use here, works well if the idiomatic usage of a VNC is sufficiently frequent compared to its literal usage. In our experiments, we examine the performance of our proposed classification methods for VNCs with different proportions of idiomatic-to-literal usages.

3 Experimental Setup

3.1 Experimental Expressions and Annotation

We use data provided by FS06, which consists of a list of VNCs and their canonical forms. From this data, we discarded expressions whose frequency in the British National Corpus[2] (BNC) is lower than 20, in an effort to make sure that there would be literal and idiomatic usages of each expression. The frequency cut-off further ensures an accurate estimate of the vectors representing each of the literal and idiomatic meanings of the expression. We also discarded expressions that were not found in at least one of two dictionaries of idioms (Seaton and Macaulay, 2002; Cowie et al., 1983). This process resulted in the selection of 60 candidate expressions.

For each of these 60 expressions, 100 sentences containing its usage were randomly selected from the automatically parsed BNC (Collins, 1999), using the automatic VNC identification method described by FS06. For an expression which occurs less than 100 times in the BNC, all of its usages were extracted. Our primary judge, a native English speaker and an author of this paper, then annotated each use of each candidate expression as one of literal, idiomatic, or unknown. When annotating a token, the judge had access to only the sentence in which it occurred, and not the surrounding sentences. If this context was insufficient to determine the class of the expression, the judge assigned the unknown label.

Idiomaticity is not a binary property, rather it is known to fall on a continuum from completely semantically transparent, or literal, to entirely opaque, or idiomatic. The human annotators were required to pick the label, literal or idiomatic, that best fit the usage in their judgment; they were not to use the unknown label for intermediate cases. Figurative extensions of literal meanings were classified as literal if their overall meaning was judged to be fairly transparent, as in *You turn right when we* ***hit the road*** *at the end of this track* (taken from the BNC). Sometimes an idiomatic usage, such as *had words* in *I was in a bad mood, and he kept pestering me, so we* ***had words***, is somewhat directly related to its literal meaning, which is not the case for more semantically opaque idioms such as *hit the roof.* The above sentence was classified as idiomatic since the idiomatic meaning is much more salient than the literal meaning.

Based on the primary judge's annotations, we removed expressions with fewer than 5 instances of either of their literal or idiomatic meanings, leaving 28 expressions. The remaining expressions were then split into development (DEV) and test (TEST) sets of 14 expressions each. The data was divided such that DEV and TEST would be approximately equal with respect to the frequency, and proportion of idiomatic-to-literal usages, of their expressions. Before consensus annotation, DEV and TEST contained a total of 813 and 743 tokens, respectively.

A second human judge, also a native English-speaking author of this paper, then annotated DEV and TEST. The observed agreement and unweighted kappa score on TEST were 76% and 0.62 respectively. The judges discussed tokens on which they disagreed to achieve a consensus annotation. Final annotations were generated by removing tokens that received the unknown label as the consensus annotation, leaving DEV and TEST with a total of 573 and 607 tokens, and an average of 41 and 43 tokens per expression, respectively.

3.2 Creation of Co-occurrence Vectors

We create co-occurrence vectors for each expression in our study from counts in the BNC. We form co-occurrence vectors for the following items.

- Each token instance of the target expression
- The target expression in its automatically determined canonical form(s)
- The target expression in its non-canonical form(s)

[2] http://www.natcorp.ox.ac.uk

- The verb in the target expression
- The noun in the target expression

The co-occurrence vectors measure the frequency with which the above items co-occur with each of 1000 *content bearing words* in the same sentence.[3] The content bearing words were chosen to be the most frequent words in the BNC which are used as a noun, verb, adjective, adverb, or determiner. Although determiners are often in a typical stoplist, we felt it would be beneficial to use them here. Determiners have been shown to be very informative in recognizing the idiomaticity of MWE types, as they are incorporated in the patterns used to automatically determine canonical forms (Fazly and Stevenson, 2006).[4]

3.3 Evaluation and Baseline

Our baseline for comparison is that of always predicting an idiomatic label, the most frequent class in our development data. We also compare our unsupervised methods against the supervised method proposed by Katz and Giesbrecht (2006). In this study, co-occurrence vectors for the tokens were formed from uses of a German idiom manually annotated as literal or idiomatic. Tokens were classified in a leave-one-out methodology using k-nearest neighbours, with $k = 1$. We report results using this method (1NN) as well as one which considers a token's 5 nearest neighbours (5NN). In all cases, we report the accuracy macro-averaged across the experimental expressions.

4 Experimental Results and Analysis

In Section 4.1, we discuss the overall performance of our proposed unsupervised methods. Section 4.2 explores possible causes of the differences observed in the performance of the methods. We examine our estimated idiomatic and literal vectors, and compare them with the actual vectors calculated from manually-annotated data. Results reported in Sections 4.1 and 4.2 are on TEST (results on DEV have very similar trends). Section 4.3 then examines the performance of the unsupervised methods on expressions with different proportions of idiomatic-to-literal usages. This section presents results on TEST and DEV combined, as explained below.

Method		%*Acc*	(%*RER*)
Baseline		61.9	-
Unsupervised	Diff$_{I\text{-}CF,\,L\text{-}Comp}$	67.8	(15.5)
	Diff$_{I\text{-}CF,\,L\text{-}NCF}$	70.1	(21.5)
	CForm	**72.4**	**(27.6)**
Supervised	1NN	72.4	(27.6)
	5NN	**76.2**	**(37.5)**

Table 1: Macro-averaged accuracy (%*Acc*) and relative error reduction (%*RER*) over TEST.

4.1 Overall Performance

Table 4.1 shows the macro-averaged accuracy on TEST of our three unsupervised methods, as well as that of the baseline and the two supervised methods for comparison (see Section 3.3). The best supervised performance and the best unsupervised performance are indicated in boldface. As the table shows, all three unsupervised methods outperform the baseline, confirming that the canonical forms of an expression, and local context, are both informative in distinguishing literal and idiomatic instances of the expression.

The table also shows that Diff$_{I\text{-}CF,\,L\text{-}NCF}$ performs better than Diff$_{I\text{-}CF,\,L\text{-}Comp}$. This suggests that estimating the literal meaning of an expression using the non-canonical forms is more accurate than using the composed vector, $\vec{v}_{L\text{-}Comp}$. In Section 4.2 we find more evidence for this. Another interesting observation is that CForm has the highest performance (among unsupervised methods), very closely followed by Diff$_{I\text{-}CF,\,L\text{-}NCF}$. These results confirm our hypothesis that canonical forms—which reflect the overall behaviour of a VNC type—are strongly informative about the class of a token, perhaps even more so than the local context of the token. Importantly, this is the case even though the canonical forms that we use are imperfect knowledge obtained automatically through an unsupervised method.

Our results using 1NN, 72.4%, are comparable

[3]We also considered 10 and 20 word windows on either side of the target expression, but experiments on development data indicated that using the sentence as a window performed better.

[4]We employed singular value decomposition (Deerwester et al., 1990) to reduce the dimensionality of the co-occurrence vectors. This had a negative effect on the results, likely because information about determiners, which occur frequently with many expressions, is lost in the dimensionality reduction.

Vectors	cosine	Vectors	cosine
$\vec{a}_{idm}$ and $\vec{a}_{lit}$	.55		
$\vec{v}_{I\text{-}CF}$ and $\vec{a}_{lit}$	.70	$\vec{v}_{I\text{-}CF}$ and $\vec{a}_{idm}$	.90
$\vec{v}_{L\text{-}NCF}$ and $\vec{a}_{lit}$	.80	$\vec{v}_{L\text{-}NCF}$ and $\vec{a}_{idm}$	.60
$\vec{v}_{L\text{-}Comp}$ and $\vec{a}_{lit}$	.72	$\vec{v}_{L\text{-}Comp}$ and $\vec{a}_{idm}$	.76

Table 2: Average similarity between the actual vectors ($\vec{a}$) and the estimated vectors ($\vec{v}$), for the idiomatic and literal meanings.

to those of Katz and Giesbrecht (2006) using this method on their German data (72%). However, their baseline is slightly lower than ours at 58%, and they only report results for 1 expression with 67 instances. Interestingly, our best unsupervised results are in line with the results using 1NN and not substantially lower than the results using 5NN.

4.2 A Closer Look into the Estimated Vectors

In this section, we compare our estimated idiomatic and literal vectors with the actual vectors for these usages calculated from manually-annotated data. Such a comparison helps explain some of the differences we observed in the performance of the methods. Table 4.2 shows the similarity between the estimated and actual vectors representing the idiomatic and literal meanings, averaged over the 14 TEST expressions. Actual vectors, referred to as $\vec{a}_{idm}$ and $\vec{a}_{lit}$, are calculated over idiomatic and literal usages of the expressions as determined by the human annotations. Estimated vectors, $\vec{v}_{I\text{-}CF}$, $\vec{v}_{L\text{-}CF}$, and $\vec{v}_{L\text{-}Comp}$, are calculated using our methods described in Section 2.2.

For comparison purposes, the first row of Table 4.2 shows the average similarity between the actual idiomatic and literal vectors, $\vec{a}_{idm}$ and $\vec{a}_{lit}$. These vectors are expected to be very dissimilar, hence the low average cosine between them serves as a baseline for comparison. We now look into the relative similarity of each estimated vector, $\vec{v}_{I\text{-}CF}$, $\vec{v}_{L\text{-}CF}$, $\vec{v}_{L\text{-}Comp}$, with these two vectors.

The second row of the table shows that, as desired, our estimated idiomatic vector, $\vec{v}_{I\text{-}CF}$, is notably more similar to the actual idiomatic vector than to the actual literal vector. Also, $\vec{v}_{L\text{-}NCF}$ is more similar to the actual literal vector than to the actual idiomatic vector (third row). Surprisingly, however, $\vec{v}_{L\text{-}Comp}$ is somewhat similar to both actual literal and idiomatic vectors (in fact it is slightly more similar to the latter). These results suggest that the vector composed of the context vectors for the constituents of an expression may not always be the best estimate of the literal meaning of the expression.[5] Given this observation, the overall better-than-baseline performance of $\text{Diff}_{I\text{-}CF,L\text{-}Comp}$ might seem unjustified at a first glance. However, we believe this performance is mainly due to an accurate estimate of $\vec{v}_{I\text{-}CF}$.

4.3 Performance Based on Class Distribution

We further divide our 28 DEV and TEST expressions according to their proportion of idiomatic-to-literal usages, as determined by the human annotators. In order to have a sufficient number of expressions in each group, here we merge DEV and TEST (we refer to the new set as DT). DTI_{high} contains 17 expressions with 65%–90% of their usages being idiomatic—i.e., their idiomatic usage is dominant. DTI_{low} contains 11 expressions with 8%–58% of their occurrences being idiomatic—i.e., their idiomatic usage is not dominant.

Table 4.3 shows the average accuracy of all the methods on these two groups of expressions, with the best performance on each group shown in boldface. On DTI_{high}, both $\text{Diff}_{I\text{-}CF,\,L\text{-}NCF}$ and CForm outperform the baseline, with CForm having the highest reduction in error rate. The two methods perform similarly to each other on DTI_{low}, though note that the error reduction of CForm is more in line with its performance on DTI_{high}. These results show that even for VNCs whose idiomatic meaning is not dominant—i.e., those in DTI_{low}—automatically-acquired canonical forms can help with their token classification.

An interesting observation in Table 4.3 is the inconsistent performance of $\text{Diff}_{I\text{-}CF,\,L\text{-}Comp}$: the method has a very poor performance on DTI_{high}, but outperforms the other two unsupervised methods on DTI_{low}. As we noted earlier in Section 2.2, the more frequent the idiomatic meaning of an expression, the more reliable the acquired canonical forms for that expression. Since the performance of CForm and $\text{Diff}_{I\text{-}CF,\,L\text{-}NCF}$ depends highly on the accuracy of the automatically acquired canonical forms, it is not surprising that these two methods perform

[5] This was also noted by Katz and Giesbrecht (2006) in their second experiment.

Method		$\text{DT}_{I_{high}}$	$\text{DT}_{I_{low}}$
Baseline		81.4 (-)	35.0 (-)
Unsuper-vised	$\text{Diff}_{I\text{-}CF,\,L\text{-}Comp}$	73.1 (-44.6)	58.6 (36.3)
	$\text{Diff}_{I\text{-}CF,\,L\text{-}NCF}$	82.3 (4.8)	52.7 (27.2)
	CForm	**84.7** (**17.7**)	53.4 (28.3)
Super-vised	1NN	78.3 (-16.7)	65.8 (47.4)
	5NN	82.3 (4.8)	**72.4** (**57.5**)

Table 3: Macro-averaged accuracy over DEV and TEST, divided according to the proportion of idiomatic-to-literal usages.

worse than $\text{Diff}_{I\text{-}CF,\,L\text{-}Comp}$ on VNCs whose idiomatic usage is not dominant.

The high performance of the supervised methods on $\text{DT}_{I_{low}}$ also confirms that the poorer performance of the unsupervised methods on these VNCs is likely due to the inaccuracy of the canonical forms extracted for them. Interestingly, when canonical forms can be extracted with a high accuracy (i.e., for VNCs in $\text{DT}_{I_{high}}$) the performance of the unsupervised methods is comparable to (or even slightly better than) that of the best supervised method. One possible way of improving the performance of unsupervised methods is thus to develop more accurate techniques for the automatic acquisition of canonical forms.

5 Related Work

Various properties of MWEs have been exploited in developing automatic identification methods for MWE types (Lin, 1999; Krenn and Evert, 2001; Fazly and Stevenson, 2006). Much research has addressed the non-compositionality of MWEs as an important property related to their idiomaticity, and has used it in the classification of both MWE types and tokens (Baldwin et al., 2003; McCarthy et al., 2003; Katz and Giesbrecht, 2006). We also make use of this property in an MWE token classification task, but in addition, we draw on other salient characteristics of MWEs which have been previously shown to be useful for their type classification (Evert et al., 2004; Fazly and Stevenson, 2006).

The idiomatic/literal token classification methods of Birke and Sarkar (2006) and Katz and Giesbrecht (2006) rely primarily on the local context of a token, and fail to exploit specific linguistic properties of non-literal language. Our results suggest that such properties are often more informative than the local context, in determining the class of an MWE token.

The supervised classifier of Patrick and Fletcher (2005) distinguishes between compositional and non-compositional English verb-particle construction tokens. Their classifier incorporates linguistically-motivated features, such as the degree of separation between the verb and particle. Here, we focus on a different class of English MWEs, verb+noun combinations. Moreover, by making a more direct use of their syntactic behaviour, we develop unsupervised token classification methods that perform well. The unsupervised token classifier of Hashimoto et al. (2006) uses manually-encoded information about allowable and non-allowable syntactic transformations of Japanese idioms—that are roughly equivalent to our notions of canonical and non-canonical forms. The rule-based classifier of Uchiyama et al. (2005) incorporates syntactic information about Japanese compound verbs (JCVs), a type of MWE composed of two verbs. In both cases, although the classifiers incorporate syntactic information about MWEs, their manual development limits the scalability of the approaches.

Uchiyama et al. (2005) also propose a statistical token classification method for JCVs. This method is similar to ours, in that it also uses type-based knowledge to determine the class of each token in context. However, their method is supervised, whereas our methods are unsupervised. Moreover, Uchiyama et al. (2005) evaluate their methods on a set of JCVs that are mostly monosemous. Here, we intentionally exclude such cases from consideration, and focus on those MWEs that have two clear idiomatic and literal meanings, and that are frequently used with either meaning.

6 Conclusions

While a great deal of research has focused on properties of MWE types, such as their compositionality, less attention has been paid to issues surrounding MWE tokens. In this study, we have developed techniques for a semantic classification of tokens of a potential MWE in context. We focus on a broadly documented class of English MWEs that are formed from the combination of a verb and a noun in its direct object position, referred to as VNCs. We annotated a total of 1180 tokens for 28 VNCs according to whether they are a literal or idiomatic usage, and we found that approximately 40% of the tokens were literal usages. These figures indicate that automatically determining whether a VNC token is used idiomatically or literally is of great importance for NLP applications. In this work, we have proposed three unsupervised methods that perform such a task. Our proposed methods incorporate automatically acquired knowledge about the overall syntactic behaviour of a VNC type, in order to do token classification. More specifically, our methods draw on the syntactic fixedness of VNCs—a property which has been largely ignored in previous studies of MWE tokens. Our results confirm the usefulness of this property as incorporated into our methods. All our methods outperform the baseline of always predicting the most frequent class. Moreover, considering our approach is unsupervised, our best accuracy of 72.4% is not substantially lower than the accuracy of a standard supervised approach at 76.2%.

References

Timothy Baldwin, Colin Bannard, Takaaki Tanaka, and Dominic Widdows. 2003. An empirical model of multiword expression decomposability. In *Proceedings of the ACL-SIGLEX Workshop on Multiword Expressions: Analysis, Acquisition and Treatment.*

Julia Birke and Anoop Sarkar. 2006. A clustering approach for nearly unsupervised recognition of nonliteral language. In *Proceedings of EACL-06*, 329–336.

Michael Collins. 1999. *Head-Driven Statistical Models for Natural Language Parsing*. Ph.D. thesis, University of Pennsylvania.

Anthony P. Cowie, Ronald Mackin, and Isabel R. McCaig. 1983. *Oxford Dictionary of Current Idiomatic English*, volume 2. Oxford University Press.

Scott C. Deerwester, Susan T. Dumais, Thomas K. Landauer, George W. Furnas, and Richard A. Harshman. 1990. Indexing by latent semantic analysis. *Journal of the American Society of Information Science*, 41(6):391–407.

Stefan Evert, Ulrich Heid, and Kristina Spranger. 2004. Identifying morphosyntactic preferences in collocations. In *Proceedings LREC-04*.

Afsaneh Fazly and Suzanne Stevenson. 2006. Automatically constructing a lexicon of verb phrase idiomatic combinations. In *Proceedings of EACL-06*, 337–344.

Christiane Fellbaum. 2002. VP idioms in the lexicon: Topics for research using a very large corpus. In S. Busemann, editor, *Proceedings of the KONVENS-02 Conference.*

John R. Firth. 1957. A synopsis of linguistic theory 1930–1955. In *Studies in Linguistic Analysis (special volume of the Philological Society)*, 1–32. The Philological Society, Oxford.

Chikara Hashimoto, Satoshi Sato, and Takehito Utsuro. 2006. Japanese idiom recognition: Drawing a line between literal and idiomatic meanings. In *Proceedings of the COLING/ACL 2006 Main Conference Poster Sessions*, 353–360.

Graham Katz and Eugenie Giesbrecht. 2006. Automatic identification of non-compositional multi-word expressions using latent semantic analysis. In *Proceedings of the ACL/COLING-06 Workshop on Multiword Expressions: Identifying and Exploiting Underlying Properties*, 12–19.

Brigitte Krenn and Stefan Evert. 2001. Can we do better than frequency? A case study on extracting PP-verb collocations. In *Proceedings of the ACL-01 Workshop on Collocations*.

Dekang Lin. 1999. Automatic identification of non-compositional phrases. In *Proceedings of ACL-99*, 317–324.

Diana McCarthy, Bill Keller, and John Carroll. 2003. Detecting a continuum of compositionality in phrasal verbs. In *Proceedings of the ACL-SIGLEX Workshop on Multiword Expressions: Analysis, Acquisition and Treatment.*

Geoffrey Nunberg, Ivan A. Sag, and Thomas Wasow. 1994. Idioms. *Language*, 70(3):491–538.

Jon Patrick and Jeremy Fletcher. 2005. Classifying verb-particle constructions by verb arguments. In *Proceedings of the Second ACL-SIGSEM Workshop on the Linguistic Dimensions of Prepositions and their use in Computational Linguistics Formalisms and Applications*, 200–209.

Ivan A. Sag, Timothy Baldwin, Francis Bond, Ann Copestake, and Dan Flickinger. 2002. Multiword expressions: A pain in the neck for NLP. In *Proceedings of CICLing-02*, 1–15.

Maggie Seaton and Alison Macaulay, editors. 2002. *Collins COBUILD Idioms Dictionary*. HarperCollins Publishers, second edition.

Kiyoko Uchiyama, Timothy Baldwin, and Shun Ishizaki. 2005. Disambiguating Japanese compound verbs. *Computer Speech and Language, Special Issue on Multiword Expressions*, 19(4):497–512.

Sriram Venkatapathy and Aravid Joshi. 2005. Measuring the relative compositionality of verb-noun (V-N) collocations by integrating features. In *Proceedings of HLT/EMNLP-05*, 899–906.

Begoña Villada Moirón and Jörg Tiedemann. 2006. Identifying idiomatic expressions using automatic word-alignment. In *Proceedings of the EACL-06 Workshop on Multiword Expressions in a Multilingual Context*, 33–40.

Pauses as an Indicator of Psycholinguistically Valid Multi-Word Expressions (MWEs)?

Irina Dahlmann and Svenja Adolphs
School of English Studies
University of Nottingham
University Park, Nottingham, NG7 2RD, UK
{aexid,svenja.adolphs}@nottingham.ac.uk

Abstract

In this paper we investigate the role of the placement of pauses in automatically extracted multi-word expression (MWE) candidates from a learner corpus. The aim is to explore whether the analysis of pauses might be useful in the validation of these candidates as MWEs. The study is based on the assumption advanced in the area of psycholinguistics that MWEs are stored holistically in the mental lexicon and are therefore produced without pauses in naturally occurring discourse. Automatic MWE extraction methods are unable to capture the criterion of holistic storage and instead rely on statistics and raw frequency in the identification of MWE candidates. In this study we explore the possibility of a combination of the two approaches. We report on a study in which we analyse the placement of pauses in various instances of two very frequent automatically extracted MWE candidates from a learner corpus, i.e. the n-grams *I don't know* and *I think I*. Intuitively, they are judged differently in terms of holistic storage. Our study explores whether pause analysis can be used as an objective empirical criterion to support this intuition. A corpus of interview data of language learners of English forms the basis of this study.

1 Introduction

MWEs are ubiquitous in language (e.g. Erman and Warren, 2001; Wray, 2002; Pawley and Syder, 2000) but at the same time they present researchers, especially in the areas of NLP, descriptive linguistics and (second) language acquisition (see for example Sag et al., 2002; Wray, 2000, 2002) with a number of challenges. Two of the most serious challenges are the identification and definition of MWEs. These are interdependent and cause a circular problem: As long as we cannot identify and describe the properties of MWEs fully, a definition remains only partial and, in return, without a full definition the identification process is incomplete.

Nevertheless, methods of identification have been developed and used, based on broad criteria, e.g. human intuition, frequency information or semantic and grammatical properties (e.g. idioms, light-verb constructions, adjective noun collocations).

A considerable amount of research in NLP and in linguistics draws on two broad definitions by Sag et al. (2002) and Wray (2002), respectively. Sag et al. define MWEs 'very roughly' as

'idiosyncratic interpretations that cross word boundaries (or spaces)' (Sag et al. 2002:2).

They specify further that MWEs can be classified broadly into two categories according to their syntactic and semantic flexibility, i.e. lexical phrases and institutionalised phrases.

Wray (2002), coming from a psycholinguistic perspective, wants to be 'as inclusive as possible, covering any kind of linguistic unit that has been considered formulaic in any research field' (p.9). She defines the term 'formulaic sequence' as

'a sequence, continuous or discontinuous, of words or other elements, which is or appears to be prefabricated: that is, stored and retrieved whole from

Proceedings of the Workshop on A Broader Perspective on Multiword Expressions, pages 49–56,
Prague, June 2007.

memory at the time of use, rather than being subject to generation or analysis by the language grammar.' (Wray 2002:9)

The main difference between the two definitions is the inclusion of holistic storage of MWEs in the mental lexicon by Wray, whereas Sag et al.'s definition, which has been used extensively in NLP research, focuses mainly on syntactic and semantic properties of the MWE.

One of the possible reasons why holistic storage has not found its way into NLP research may be related to the fact that this criterion is almost impossible to measure directly. However, it has been proposed that prosodic cues and pauses are indirect indicators of prefabricated language and holistic storage as MWEs in speech exhibit more phonological coherence (e.g. Hickey, 1993).

If we assume that MWEs are stored as holistic units in memory, we would firstly not expect to find pauses *within* MWEs. Pawley (1986) states that 'pauses within lexicalised phrase are less acceptable than pauses within free expressions, and after a hesitation the speaker is more likely to restart from the beginning of the expression' (p.107, quoted from Wray, 2002). This is in line with Raupach (1984) who studied spontaneous L2 speech production and stresses that 'a formal approach to identifying formula units in spontaneous speech must, as a first step, list the strings which are not interrupted by unfilled pauses' (p.116).

Secondly, we would expect that pauses, i.e. silent pauses and hesitation phenomena, may also serve in the delineation of MWE boundaries (Raupach, 1984:114).

The research outlined above is echoed in more recent studies of MWEs and pauses in the development of speech fluency. The placement, quantity and lengths of pauses are important markers of fluency (e.g. Riggenbach 1991) and the stretches between pauses may be fluent because pauses provide planning time to formulate the next utterance (Pawley and Syder, 2000) and the utterance may be (partly) a prefabricated string of words (MWE).

Previous research into MWEs and fluency is especially important from a methodological perspective, as it provides methodological frameworks for the study of pauses, for example, the integration of silent and filled pauses, which both provide planning time (Raupach, 1984; Pawley and Syder, 2000), or the significance of pause lengths (Pawley and Syder, 2000). These aspects are, for instance, not sufficiently reflected in existing pause annotation schemes in spoken corpora (see also section 3.1), which has hampered the study of pauses and MWEs on a large scale so far.

The aim of our study is therefore twofold. Firstly, in terms of methodology, we combine insights from fluency and MWEs research with a corpus approach and automatic extraction of MWEs.

Secondly, we analyse whether units which have been extracted automatically also comply with predicted pause behaviour (no pauses within MWEs, pauses as indicator of MWE boundaries) and therefore whether they are psycholinguistically valid.

This kind of study may help develop our understanding of MWEs in naturally occurring discourse. In addition, it allows us to explore further whether the study of pause phenomena might be a useful tool in the evaluation of automatic extraction methods.

2 Pauses and MWEs

As outlined above research on prosodic features and MWEs has found that MWEs tend to exhibit more phonological coherence (e.g. Hickey, 1993; Read and Nation 2004; Wray, 2002). Van Lancker et al. (1981), for instance, found phonological differences depending on whether a string carried literal or idiomatic meaning in a read aloud task (e.g. *skating on thin ice*). The differences in the literal and idiomatic contexts were partly mirrored in the number and placement of pauses. Idiomatic expressions are uttered at a faster speed which is to some extent related to the lack of pauses within the idiomatic expression (Van Lancker et al. 1981:331). Additional indicators are the pace at which key words were used (increased word duration of major lexical items in the literal version), the length of the whole utterance, pitch changes, and articulatory precision (Van Lancker et al., 1981). Phonological coherence and further prosodic features (stress and intonation) may therefore be regarded as physical indicators of the storage and retrieval of MWEs which in turn can help to identify MWEs in spoken language.

Problems with this kind of investigation are mainly related to the lack of consistent methodology for studying pauses as physical markers of holistic storage in an empirical manner, i.e. using naturally occurring corpus data. Key problems are the shortage of suitable spoken corpora and inconsistent pause annotation schemes.

3 Methodological challenges

3.1 Corpora and pause annotation

As the aim of this study is to explore holistic storage and retrieval of MWEs in naturally occurring speech, a corpus of spontaneous speech is required. Both, audio data and transcriptions are needed for the automatic extraction of MWEs and pause annotation respectively.

Unfortunately, not many available spoken corpora have been marked up for pauses as it is a very labour intensive process and currently has to be done largely manually. In cases where pause marking has been applied, it does not necessarily meet the specific requirements for phonological analysis (Read & Nation 2004:32). For example, pauses may not have been defined sufficiently for this purpose, as in the spoken part of the BNC where a pause is defined as a 'silence, within or between utterances, longer than was judged normal for the speaker or speakers' [1]. The definition of pause length – unlike in fluency research – can be too broad in existing corpus annotation, e.g. pauses have to be perceived as a pause (short, medium, long) or, when timing is included it is often very vague, e.g. a 'comma indicates a brief (1-2 second) mid-utterance pause with non-phrase final intonation contour' in the MICASE corpus.[2] In comparison, the minimum threshold for a pause lies at around 0.2-0.3 seconds in fluency research. Furthermore, not all corpora which contain silent pause annotation have also annotated filled pauses. In fact, a survey of 12 corpus pause coding schemes (native and learner language) shows that none complies with the requirements needed for the study of fluency and MWU related research.[3]

Due to the lack of corpora which combine spontaneous speech and appropriate pause annotation we have developed a learner corpus which we then selectively annotated for pauses. The corpus contains 290,000 transcribed words of spontaneous interview discourse produced by Chinese learners of English (with accompanying audio files). The proficiency level of the Chinese students in the whole corpus is based on IELTS scores and ranges from 5.0 – 6.5 (of max. 9). Scores from around 5.5 onwards (depending on the intended studies) are required for foreign students for admission at a British university. The two speakers investigated here have scores of 5.0 and 5.5 respectively.

Only two students have been chosen for this study in order to reduce the number of possible variables affecting the results, especially with regard to idiosyncratic usage.

The choice of learner data rather than native speaker data evolved not only from practical considerations, but also from the wider aim of our study which is related to fluency and language acquisition. In addition, when applying preliminary pause annotations to extracts of both native and non-native speech, we observed that learners seem to pause a lot more than native speakers. Native speakers seem to apply some other modes of 'pausing' – such as using fillers, repeating words or rephrasing – more extensively. Therefore, we might expect clearer results from the learner data initially. In fact, it will be interesting to see in comparison, whether pauses might even tell us more about learners than about native speakers with regard to the use of MWEs.

It nevertheless has to be acknowledged that there might be considerable differences in learner and native speech; however, both varieties are valid in their own right, especially with respect to holistic storage and usage.

Careful pause annotation was then carried out around a selected set of automatically extracted MWEs from the learner data (see 3.2 and 3.3) to explore the approach outlined above.

3.2 Automatic extraction – n-grams

Different MWE extraction methods abound but we decided to begin our study with an investigation of n-grams as a way into the proposed ap-

[1] http://www.natcorp.ox.ac.uk/docs/userManual/cdif.xml.ID=cdifsp (last accessed 25/03/2007)

[2] http://www.lsa.umich.edu/eli/micase/MICASE_MANUAL.pdf (last accessed 25/03/2007)

[3] This is especially unfortunate in the case of the London-Lund Corpus (LLC), which in theory lends itself to this kind of study for native English MWEs usage: The LLC contains not only pause annotation but also marking of other prosodic features such as tone unit boundaries, the nucleus, and varying degrees of stress. These can serve as additional indicators for MWEs in use. However, only silent pauses are marked and only in broad terms, i.e. '-' indicates a 'brief pause of one light syllable', '–' indicates a 'unit pause of one stress unit or 'foot'. This is one of the limitations of the only large-scale study in the field of pauses and MWEs (Erman, 2007), as it is based solely on the LLC and its annotation.

proach. The choice of n-grams, described as one of the most successful statistical models (Gil and Dias, 2003), was based on several reasons.

Firstly, the assumption behind n-grams is that continuous strings of words, which are used repeatedly and frequently in the same form in a speech community, are also likely to be stored holistically in memory.

Secondly, simple n-grams are continuous sequences. This aids the study of pauses at this early stage as discontinuous sequences or sequences with variable slots might exhibit different pause behaviour and/or prosodic features.[4]

In addition, the special case of learner language requires an extraction method which is based on the actual corpus data itself and not on preconceived ideas of whether or not a particular multi-word string is in fact a valid MWE, as is the case with symbolic or knowledge based extraction methods. Learners may have their own (sub-)set of MWEs (Wray 1999). These may be characterised by idiosyncratic MWEs, which nevertheless may be used frequently either by individuals or by a certain speech community, e.g. Chinese learners of English.

A further advantage of using n-grams is that the extraction is fully automated and therefore does not require human intervention. This extraction method does not take into account the additional factor of 'meaning' as the process of extraction itself is very mechanical and not dependant on meaning.

N	3-grams	Freq.	%
1	A LOT OF	352	0.17
2	**I DON'T KNOW**	**327**	**0.16**
3	**I THINK I**	**300**	**0.15**
4	I THINK IT'S	252	0.12
5	SO I THINK	220	0.11
6	I WANT TO	211	0.1
7	I THINK THE	188	0.09
8	BUT I THINK	185	0.09
9	I DON'T THINK	146	0.07
10	I THINK ER	143	0.07

Table 1. 10 most frequent 3-grams extracted from 290,000 words of learner interview data

[4] Discontinuous MWEs and n-grams are nevertheless important, which is reflected in the development of more refined extraction methods (e.g. positional n-grams (Gil and Dias, 2003) and ConcGrams (Chen et al. 2006)). However, they are only of secondary interest for us at this stage.

This is one of the disadvantages at the same time. Frequent examples in our spoken learner corpus are n-grams such as *I think er*, *I I I* or *and er I* which at first glance do not appear to be holistically stored MWEs.

Drawing on n-grams as an approach also allows us to study MWE candidates, which – on the basis of intuition – do not appear to be stored holistically, but nevertheless occur very frequently in the corpus.

For our analysis we have chosen two very frequent 3-grams (see Table 1) which contrast in terms of their internal consistency. *I don't know* seems to be an example of a self contained MWE candidate whereas *I think I* is an example of a MWE candidate which intuitively does not seem to be psycholinguistically valid, i.e. stored as a holistic item.[5]

3.3 Pause annotation and research questions

The analysis has been carried out for two different speakers and the following number of n-grams (see Table 2).

MWE candidate	Speaker MS001	Speaker MS003
I don't know	21	26
I think I	16	28

Table 2. MWE candidates per speaker

Pauses have been measured manually with audio-visual clues, i.e. the combination of audio recording and waveforms, both displayed by Adobe Audition. Within this software the pause length (in seconds, correct to the third decimal) is calculated by marking up a stretch of the wave form, which has been identified as a pause.

[5] The analysis of other contrastive pairs, e.g. on the basis of syntactic properties such as *I don't know* vs. *I don't see* (keeping the syntactic structure but changing the lexical verb - as suggested by one of the reviewers) also seems sensible. However, the choice of the substituting items has to be well informed by factors such as frequency of the single lexical verbs, compared to frequency of the whole string, as for example done by Tremblay et al. (2007). However, this does not necessarily lead to an unproblematic comparison: *I don't see*, for instance, only occurs two times in our data set of spontaneous speech, which is not frequent enough to find pause patterns or to compare it to the pause patterns of *I don't know*. Such an approach thus seems to lend itself more readily to experimental studies (such as the self-paced reading experiments by Tremblay et al. 2007) with carefully designed stimuli, and not to the study of natural occurring speech.

Pause measurement in fluency research commonly suggests thresholds between 0.2-0.3 seconds as a minimum for a silence to be regarded and perceived as a pause (e.g. Goldman Eisler, 1968, Towell et al., 1996). To account for this, pauses between 0.2 and 0.3 seconds length were measured correct to two digits in order to allow for a later adjustment of minimal pause length, pauses above 0.3 were measured to one digit. Filled pauses were measured if they seemed exceptionally long. Both, silent and filled pauses are marked here for the purpose of placement indication with ‘< >’.

The main focus of our analysis is on pause distribution and the following five cases of placements of pauses have been identified as pertinent to our study: (‘____‘indicates text which can theoretically be of any length, < > indicates pause)

a. M W < > E (pause within the MWE candidate)
b. < > MWE < >
c. < > MWE ____< >
d. < > _____MWE < >
e. < > _____MWE _____ < >

In the annotation of pause patterns around the two different MWE candidates the following questions are explored:

(1) Do the two candidates seem to be stored holistically, i.e. do they contain pauses within the extracted form or not? (Referring to pause placement pattern a.)

(2) Do pauses assist in the determination of MWE boundaries, i.e. are there any regular pause patterns which indicate boundaries? Do pauses seem to align MWEs in the form in which they were extracted? (Referring to b.-e.)

(3) Do the results comply with intuition, i.e. does *I don’t know* fit the predicted behaviour better than *I think I*?

4 Results and discussion

4.1 ‘I don’t know’

Forty seven *I don’t know*’s, used by two different speakers within approximately 71,000 words of interview data have been studied for pause phenomena. The distribution is summarised in Table 3.

Pause distribution	**MS001**	**MS003**	**Σ**
MW< > E	--	--	**--**
< > MWE < >	9	1	**10**
< > MWE __ < >	5	14	**19**
< > __ MWE < >	2	3	**5**
< > __ MWE__ < >	5	8	**13**

Table 3. Pause distribution around 47 instances of *I don’t know*

As expected, in the speech examples at hand, *I don’t know* is never interrupted by pauses, which is a good indicator for holistic storage of this particular string of words by the two learners.

In terms of boundary alignments it can be observed that almost two thirds of the examples contain pauses immediately preceding *I don’t know* (29:18), which in turn can be interpreted as a sign of a MWE boundary. It has to bc taken into account that MWEs can occur within other MWEs or within a stretch of creative speech. Therefore, pauses do not need to be present on all occasions even if it seems to be a boundary. The fact, that pauses nevertheless do occur very often and that these pauses are proper pauses - on average far longer than the suggested 0.2 seconds (on average 0.57 seconds) reinforces the case for an actual boundary.

The case is different for the final boundary. If pauses occur right at the end of *I don’t know* they are shorter overall (0.39 seconds on average). The main point is, however, that in over two thirds of the instances (32:15) no pause occurs in this place.

A further observation is that the ‘ideal’ form (in terms of boundary recognition and validation) < > MWE < > with pauses at either side of the extracted MWE candidate, occurs infrequently. It seems rather idealistic to expect language to be organized neatly according to stored chunks. Instead speakers are generally capable of placing several chunks and/or creative language together in one stretch of speech. Pawley and Syder (2000) suggest that ‘the average number of words per fluent unit is about six’ (p. 195) for fluent (native) speakers. The actual average number of words might differ slightly for learners, however the point is that either way the numbers are averages and in single instances stretches might be considerably longer. It is therefore not surprising that 3-word n-grams might be embedded within longer stretches of speech and are not surrounded by pauses. Furthermore, Miller (1956) states in his paper *The magical number seven*, that 'the memory span is a fixed number of chunks, we can increase the number of bits of information that it contains simply by building larger and larger chunks, each chunk containing more information than before.' (p.93). In other words, if *I don't know* is stored as one chunk or item (instead of three single words) it is more likely that it may be embedded in a larger portion of language as the memory is able to handle more language items.

Moreover, the form < > MWE < > is mainly used by one speaker (MS001; 9:1). This points towards the importance of the consideration of idiosyncratic usage, especially when dealing with learner language (but it also plays a role in native usage): learners may use MWEs in a much more restricted way, i.e. the way they have learned a particular phrase instead of using it appropriate to the context. For instance, learner MS003 evidently also has a preferred way of using *I don't know*, namely < > MWE __ < > (14:5).

It also has to be taken into consideration that *I don't know* can be used as a discourse marker/filler or in the more literal sense of 'I don't have the knowledge'. This distinction might be of significance for clearer descriptions of the MWE generally.

In summary, one may want to argue that *I don't know* may function as a core MWE. It seems to be stored holistically as it does not exhibit pauses within the core, but it allows for variation and elongation at the end, preferably introduced by a question word (e.g. why, what, where, how). For example, four out of five instances of speaker MS001, using the form < > I don't know __ < >, are followed by *why*. Speaker MS003 also prefers why (in 6 out of 14 instances). That raises the question as to whether *I dont know why* may even be regarded as a separate MWE. In fact, considering all results and the distribution of pauses, one could also argue that there may be several different MWEs:

- I don't know
- I don't know wh=
- I don't know why
- I don't know why but
- I don't know if
- I don't know [the (NP)]
- but I don't know

Biber et al. (1999:1002), studying *lexical bundles*[6] also found plenty of such structures. For example, they find that the structure *personal pronoun + lexical verb phrase (+ complement–clause fragment)* - which fits most of the above examples – is very common in conversation. They also record many of the examples listed above in their category of four-word bundle expressions with *I + know.* (ibid.). However, whereas their analysis is based on frequency information alone, the very rare use of pauses between *I don't know* and the subsequent word(s) gives more confidence in that these strings are actually valid units from *two* perspective, that of frequency and holistic storage.

4.2 'I think I'

Forty four instances of *I think I* have been annotated. The pause distribution within these examples is as follows:

Pause distribution	MS001	MS003	Σ
MW< > E	5	3	**8**
< > MWE < >	1	3	**4**
< > MWE __ < >	5	7	**12**
< > __ MWE < >	--	3	**3**
< > __ MWE__ < >	5	12	**17**

Table 4. Pause distribution around 44 instances of *I think I*

I think I had been chosen for analysis because – intuitively – it does not seem to be a holistically stored MWE. Especially in comparison with no single pause occurring within 47 *I don't know's* the results seem to (at least partly) confirm this. Eight out of 44 examples do exhibit pause phenomena in *I think I* which is a first indicator that probably not all instances of *I think I* are stored holistically. A closer assessment of the eight MW< >E instances reveals that all but one exhibit the pause after *I think.* This is not surprising as *I think* is the most frequent occurring bi-gram in the data (almost 3000 instances in the 290,000 word learner corpus and 3 times more frequent as the second most frequent bi-gram *you know*). In fact, *I think I* could be regarded as a sub-unit of *I think*, similar to the relationship between *I don't know* and *I don't know*

[6] The definition of lexical bundles is essentially based on frequency - they are 'sequences of words that most commonly co-occur in a register.' Furthermore, Biber et al. observed that 'most lexical bundles are not structurally complete at all' (Biber et al. 1999:989).

why. Thus, the eight instances with pause breaks may be actually instances of the MWE candidate *I know* where *I* happens to mark the beginning of the next clause.

Interestingly, all 44 instances are followed by a full clause, which has the second *I* of *I think I* as the subject at the beginning of the new clause. In addition, *I think* seems to be used rather in the function of filler, possibly in order to provide *thinking* time for the next utterance. This happens extensively in the eight *I think* < > *I*____ cases where *I think* is followed by a pause. However, and as discussed earlier, the absence of a pause does not necessarily mean the absence of a MWE boundary. Therefore the 17 < > __ I think I __ < > cases and the 12 < > I think I __ < > cases may follow the same pattern with using *I think* as a filler. In these instances no further pause is necessary. However, this does not explain the 7 instances where pauses do occur at the end of *I think I*. Idiosyncratic usage might be one explanation as it is mainly a feature used by MS003 (6 times) and the only instance of MS001 coincides with a false start. Further investigations using a larger data-set might be able to confirm whether this pattern is due to idiosyncratic usage.

4.3 Summary and limitations

The analysis of pauses in our data would suggest that *I don't know* might be stored holistically while it is questionable that this is the case for *I think I* which is interrupted by pauses in some of the instances that were investigated.

In terms of the delineation of boundaries, it can be said that pauses are only helpful to a limited extent as boundaries are not conditional on them. The absence of a pause does not exclude the possibility that it might in fact be a boundary. However, where pauses occur they give valuable indications of possible boundaries. The results can give useful information on actual MWE usage to fields such as lexicography, (second/computational) language acquisition and teaching.

These initial findings are encouraging, but they are nevertheless based on limited data in terms of the number and forms of MWEs investigated, and also the number of speakers considered.

Future research should thus draw on more instances by different speakers in order to determine idiosyncratic usage and to arrive at more stable patterns. A comparison with native speaker usage seems crucial and promising for a more comprehensive description of MWEs.

In addition, studying intonation and stress patterns of these instances may indicate boundaries more clearly.

Finally, MWEs may be used in more than one sense, as in the case of *I don't know* which has to be considered for each different MWE candidate individually.

5 Conclusion: Value for NLP and future work

In this paper we have reported on a study which combines approaches within NLP for the identification of MWE candidates with pause analysis. The aim was to explore an approach which might lead to a frequency-based and psycholinguistically motivated description of MWEs.

The results of our study seem to suggest that the placement of pauses might be valuable as an additional criterion for the identification of holistically stored MWEs, however, larger data-sets and further pause annotation is necessary to confirm our initial findings.

Further investigations of other functions of pauses and other prosodic features within a given stretch of discourse need to be carried out in order to fully assess the role of pauses in relation to holistic storage. A discourse functional analysis would be necessary to identify functional motivation of pauses and to delineate these from n-grams where the placement of pauses is related to holistic storage.

However, our study has illustrated the potential of a multi-method and interdisciplinary approach to the identification and description of MWEs which may eventually be necessary to overcome some of the problems within NLP in terms of developing extraction methods, and some of the problems in descriptive linguistics and discourse analysis in terms of gathering evidence for different MWEs in use.

Acknowledgement

The research described in this paper is supported by the Engineering and Physical Science Research Council (EPSRC, grant EP/C548191/1). We would also like to thank the three anonymous reviewers for their comments on an earlier draft of this paper.

References

Douglas Biber, Stig Johansson, Geoffrey Leech, Susan Conrad and Edward Finegan. 1999. *Longman Grammar of spoken and written English*. Harlow: Longman

Winnie Chen, Chris Greaves and Martin Warren. 2006. From n-gram to skipgram to concgram. *International Journal of Corpus Linguistics* 11(4): 411-433.

Britt Erman. 2007. Cognitive processes as evidence of the idiom principle. *International Journal of Corpus Linguistics* 12(1): 25-53.

Britt Erman and Beatrice Warren. 2000. The idiom principle and the open choice principle. *Text* 20(1): 29-62.

Alexandre Gil and Gaël Dias. 2003. Using Masks, Suffix Array-based Data Structures and Multidimensional Arrays to Compute Positional Ngram Statistics from Corpora. In: Proceedings of the ACL 2003 'Workshop on Multiword Expressions: Analysis, Acquisition and Treatment', Sapporo, Japan 12th July 2003, 25-32.

Frieda Goldman-Eisler. 1968. *Psycholinguistics: experiments in spontaneous speech*. London, New York: Academic Press.

Tina Hickey. 1993. Identifying formulas in first language acquisition. *Journal of Child Language* 20:27-41.

George A Miller. 1956. The magical number seven, plus or minus two: some limits on our capacity for processing information. *The Psychological Review* 63(2):81-97.

Andrew Pawley. 1986. *Lexicalization*. In: Deborah Tannen and James E. Alatis (eds.). Language & Linguistics: The interdependence of theory, data & application. Georgetown University Round Table on Languages & Linguistics 1985, 98-120.

Andrew Pawley and Frances Syder. 2000. *The One-Clause-at-a-Time Hypothesis*. In: Heidi Riggenbach (ed.). Perspectives on fluency. Ann Arbor: University of Michigan Press, 163-199.

Manfred Raupach. 1984. *Formulae in Second Language Speech Production*. In: Hans W. Dechert, Dorothea Möhle and Manfred Raupach (eds.). Second Language Productions. Tübingen: Narr, 114-137.

John Read and Paul Nation. 2004. *Measurement of formulaic sequences*. In: Norbert Schmitt (ed.). Formulaic Sequences. Amsterdam: John Benjamins, 23-35.

Heidi Riggenbach. 1991. Towards an understanding of fluency: A microanalysis of nonnative speaker conversations. *Discourse Processes,* 14: 423-441.

Ivan Sag, Timothy Baldwin, Francis Bond, Ann Copestake and Dan Flickinger. 2002. *Multiword expressions: A Pain in the Neck for NLP*. In: Proceedings of the 3rd International Conferences on Intelligent Text Processing and Computational Linguistics (CICLing-2002), Mexico City, Mexico, 1-15.

Antoine Tremblay, Bruce Derwing, Gary Libben and Chris Westbury. 2007. *Are Lexical Bundles Stored and Processed as Single Units?* Paper presented at the 25th UWM Linguistics Symposium on Formulaic Language. Milwaukee, Wisconsin, April 18-21, 2007

Richard Towell, Roger Hawkins and Nives Bazergui 1996. The development of fluency in advanced learners of French. *Applied Linguistics,* 17(1):84-119.

Diana Van Lancker, Gerald J. Canter and Dale Terbeek. 1981. Disambiguation of Ditropic Sentences: Acoustic and Phonetic Cues. *Journal of Speech and Hearing Research*, 24:330-335.

Alison Wray. 2002. *Formulaic Language and the Lexicon*. Cambridge, CUP.

Alison Wray. 1999. Formulaic language in learners and native speakers. *Language Teaching*, 32:213-231.

Co-occurrence Contexts for Noun Compound Interpretation

Diarmuid Ó Séaghdha
Computer Laboratory
University of Cambridge
15 JJ Thomson Avenue
Cambridge CB3 0FD
United Kingdom
do242@cl.cam.ac.uk

Ann Copestake
Computer Laboratory
University of Cambridge
15 JJ Thomson Avenue
Cambridge CB3 0FD
United Kingdom
aac10@cl.cam.ac.uk

Abstract

Contextual information extracted from corpora is frequently used to model semantic similarity. We discuss distinct classes of context types and compare their effectiveness for compound noun interpretation. Contexts corresponding to word-word similarity perform better than contexts corresponding to relation similarity, even when relational co-occurrences are extracted from a much larger corpus. Combining word-similarity and relation-similarity kernels further improves SVM classification performance.

1 Introduction

The compound interpretation task is frequently cast as the problem of classifying an unseen compound noun with one of a closed set of relation categories. These categories may consist of lexical paraphrases, such as the prepositions of Lauer (1995), or deeper semantic relations, such as the relations of Girju et al. (2005) and those used here. The challenge lies in the fact that by their very nature compounds do not give any surface realisation to the relation that holds between their constituents. To identify the difference between *bread knife* and *steel knife* it is not sufficient to assign correct word-senses to *bread*, *steel* and *knife*; it is also necessary to reason about how the entities referred to interact in the world. A common assumption in data-driven approaches to the problem is that compounds with semantically similar constituents will encode similar relations. If a hearer knows that a *fish knife* is a *knife used to eat fish*, he/she might conclude that the novel compound *pigeon fork* is a *fork used to eat pigeon* given that *pigeon* is similar to *fish* and *knife* is similar to *fork*. A second useful intuition is that word pairs which co-occur in similar contexts are likely to enter into similar relations.

In this paper, we apply these insights to identify different kinds of contextual information that capture different kinds of similarity and compare their applicability using medium- to large-sized corpora. In keeping with most other research on the problem,[1] we take a supervised learning approach to compound interpretation.

2 Defining Contexts for Compound Interpretation

When extracting corpus information to interpret a compound such as *bread knife*, there are a number of context types that might plausibly be of interest:

1. The contexts in which instances of the compound type appear (type similarity); e.g., all sentences in the corpus that contain the compound *bread knife*.
2. The contexts in which instances of each constituent appear (word similarity); e.g., all sentences containing the word *bread* or the word *knife*.
3. The contexts in which both constituents appear together (relation similarity); e.g., all sentences containing both *bread* and *knife*.
4. The context in which the particular compound token was found (token similarity).

[1] Such as Girju et al. (2005), Girju (2006), Turney (2006). Lapata and Keller's (2004) unsupervised approach is a notable exception.

Proceedings of the Workshop on A Broader Perspective on Multiword Expressions, pages 57–64,
Prague, June 2007.

A simple but effective method for exploiting these contexts is to count features that co-occur with the target items in those contexts. Co-occurrence may be defined in terms of proximity in the text, lexical patterns, or syntactic patterns in a parse graph. We can parameterise our notion of context further, for example by enforcing a constraint that the co-occurrence correspond to a particular type of grammatical relation or that co-occurrence features belong to a particular word class.[2]

Research in NLP frequently makes use of one or more of these similarity types. For example, Culotta and Sorensen (2004) combine word similarity and relation similarity for relation extraction; Gliozzo et al. (2005) combine word similarity and token similarity for word sense disambiguation. Turney (2006) discusses word similarity (which he calls "attributional similarity") and relation similarity, but focusses on the latter and does not perform a comparative study of the kind presented here.

The experiments described here investigate type, word and relation similarity. However, token similarity clearly has a role to play in the interpretation task, as a given compound type can have a different meaning in different contexts – for example, a *school book* can be *a book used in school*, *a book belonging to a school* or *a book about a school*. As our data have been annotated in context, we intend to model this dynamic in future work.

3 Experimental Setup

3.1 Data

We used the dataset of 1443 compounds whose development is described in Ó Séaghdha (2007). These compounds have been annotated in their sentential contexts using the six deep semantic relations listed in Table 1. On the basis of a dual-annotator study, Ó Séaghdha reports agreement of 66.2% ($\hat{\kappa} = 0.62$) on a more general task of annotating a noisy corpus and estimated agreement of 73.6% ($\hat{\kappa} = 0.68$) on annotating the six relations used here. These figures are superior to previously reported results on annotating compounds extracted from corpora. Always choosing the most frequent class (IN) would give accuracy of 21.34%, and we use this as a baseline for our experiments.

Relation	Distribution	Example
BE	191 (13.24%)	*steel knife, elm tree*
HAVE	199 (13.79%)	*street name, car door*
IN	308 (21.34%)	*forest hut, lunch time*
INST	266 (18.43%)	*rice cooker, bread knife*
ACTOR	236 (16.35%)	*honey bee, bus driver*
ABOUT	243 (16.84%)	*fairy tale, history book*

Table 1: The 6 relation classes and their distribution in the dataset

3.2 Corpus

The written section of the British National Corpus,[3] consisting of around 90 million words, was used in all our experiments. This corpus is not large compared to other corpora used in NLP, but it has been manually compiled with a view to a balance of genre and should be more representative of the language in general than corpora containing only newswire text. Furthermore, the compound dataset was also extracted from the BNC and information derived from it will arguably describe the data items more accurately than information from other sources. However, this information may be very sparse given the corpus' size. For comparison we also use a 187 million word subset of the English Gigaword Corpus (Graff, 2003) to derive relational information in Section 6. This subset consists of every paragraph in the Gigaword Corpus belonging to articles tagged as 'story' and containing both constituents of a compound in the dataset, whether or not they are compounded there. Both corpora were lemmatised, tagged and parsed with RASP (Briscoe et al., 2006).

3.3 Learning Algorithm

In all our experiments we use a one-against-all implementation of the Support Vector Machine.[4] Except for the work described in Section 6.2 we used the linear kernel $K(x, y) = x \cdot y$ to compute similarity between vector representations of the data items. The linear kernel consistently achieved superior performance to the more flexible Gaussian kernel in a range tests, presumably due to the sensitivity of

[2] A flexible framework for this kind of context definition is presented by Padó and Lapata (2003).

[3] `http://www.natcorp.ox.ac.uk/`

[4] The software used was LIBSVM (Chang and Lin, 2001).

the Gaussian kernel to its parameter settings.[5] One-against-all classification (training one classifier per class) performed better than one-against-one (training one classifier for each pair of classes). We estimate test accuracy by 5-fold cross-validation and within each fold we perform further 5-fold cross-validation on the training set to optimise the single SVM parameter C. An advantage of the linear kernel is that learning is very efficient. The optimisation, training and testing steps for each fold take from less than a minute on a single processor for the sparsest feature vectors to a few hours for the most dense, and the folds can easily be distributed across machines.

4 Word Similarity

Ó Séaghdha (2007) investigates the effectiveness of word-level co-occurrences for compound interpretation, and the results presented in this section are taken from that paper. Co-occurrences were identified in the BNC for each compound constituent in the dataset, using the following context definitions:

win5, win10: Each word within a window of 5 or 10 words on either side of the item is a feature.

Rbasic, Rmod, Rverb, Rconj: These feature sets use the grammatical relation output of the RASP parser run over the written BNC. The **Rbasic** feature set conflates information about 25 grammatical relations; **Rmod** counts only prepositional, nominal and adjectival noun modification; **Rverb** counts only relations among subjects, objects and verbs; **Rconj** counts only conjunctions of nouns.

The feature vector for each target constituent counts its co-occurrences with the 10,000 words that most frequently appear in the co-occurrence relations of interest over the entire corpus. A feature vector for each compound was created by appending the vectors for its modifier and head, and these compound vectors were used for SVM learning. To model aspects of co-occurrence association that might be obscured by raw frequency, the log-likelihood ratio G^2 (Dunning, 1993) was also used to transform the feature space.

[5] Keerthi and Lin (2003) prove that the Gaussian kernel will always do as well as or better than the linear kernel for binary classification. For multiclass classification we use multiple binary classifiers with a shared set of parameters which may not be optimal for any single classifier.

	Raw		G^2	
	Accuracy	Macro	Accuracy	Macro
w5	52.60%	51.07%	51.35%	49.93%
w10	51.84%	50.32%	50.10%	48.60%
Rbasic	51.28%	49.92%	51.83%	50.26%
Rmod	51.35%	50.06%	48.51%	47.03%
Rverb	48.79%	47.13%	48.58%	47.07%
Rconj	**54.12%**	**52.44%**	**54.95%**	**53.42%**

Table 2: Classification results for word similarity

Micro- and macro-averaged performance figures are given in Table 2. The micro-averaged figure is calculated as the overall proportion of items that were classified correctly, whereas the macro-average is calculated as the average of the accuracy on each class and thus balances out any skew in the class distribution. In all cases macro-accuracy is lower than micro-accuracy; this is due to much better performance on the relations IN, INST, ACTOR and ABOUT than on BE and HAVE. This may be because those two relations are slightly rarer and hence provide less training data, or it may reflect a difference in the suitability of co-occurrence data for their classification. It is interesting that features derived only from conjunctions give the best performance; these features are the most sparse but appear to be of high quality. The information contained in conjunctions is conceptually very close to the WordNet-derived information frequently used in word-similarity based approaches to compound semantics, and the performance of these features is not far off the 56.76% accuracy (54.6% macro-average) reported for WordNet-based classification for the same dataset by Ó Séaghdha (2007).

5 Type Similarity

Type similarity is measured by identifying co-occurrences with each instance of the compound type in the corpus. In effect, we are treating compounds as single words and calculating their word similarity with each other. The same feature extraction methods were used as in the previous section. Classification results are given in Table 3.

This method performs very poorly. Sparsity is undoubtedly a factor: 513 of the 1,443 compounds oc-

	Accuracy	Macro
win5	28.62%	27.71%
win10	**30.01%**	**28.69%**
Rbasic	29.31%	28.22%
Rmod	26.54%	25.30%
Rverb	25.02%	23.96%
Rconj	24.60%	24.48%

Table 3: Classification results for type similarity

cur 5 times or fewer in the BNC and 186 occur just once. The sparser feature sets (**Rmod**, **Rverb** and **Rconj**) are all outperformed by the more dense ones. However, there is also a conceptual problem with type similarity, in that the context of a compound may contain information about the referent of the compound but is less likely to contain information about the implicit semantic relation. For example, the following compounds all encode different meanings but are likely to appear in similar contexts:

- John cut the bread with the *kitchen knife*.
- John cut the bread with the *steel knife*.
- John cut the bread with the *bread knife*.

6 Relation Similarity

6.1 Vector Space Kernels

The intuition underlying the use of relation similarity is that while the relation between the constituents of a compound may not be made explicit in the context of that compound, it may be described in other contexts where both constituents appear. For example, sentences containing both *bread* and *knife* may contain information about the typical interactions between their referents. To extract feature vectors for each constituent pair, we took the maximal context unit to be each sentence in which both constituents appear, and experimented with a range of refinements to that context definition. The resulting definitions are given below in order of intuitive richness, from measures based on word-counting to measures making use of the structure of the sentence's dependency parse graph.

allwords All words in the sentence are co-occurrence features. This context may be parameterised by specifying a limit on the window size to the left of the leftmost constituent and to the right of the rightmost constituent i.e., the words between the two constituents are always counted.

midwords All words between the constituents are counted.

allGRs All words in the sentence entering into a grammatical relation (with any other word) are counted. This context may be parameterised by specifying a limit on the length of the shortest path in the dependency graph from either of the target constituents to the feature word.

shortest path All words on the shortest dependency path between the two constituents are features. If there is no such path, no features are extracted.

path triples The shortest dependency path is decomposed into a set of triples and these triples are used as features. Each triple consists of a node on the shortest path (the triple's centre node) and two edges connecting that node with other nodes in the parse graph (not necessarily nodes on the path). To generate further triple features, one or both of the off-centre nodes is replaced by part(s) of speech. For example, the RASP dependency parse of *The knife cut the fresh bread* is:

```
(|ncsubj| |cut:3_VVD| |knife:2_NN1| _)
(|dobj| |cut:3_VVD| |bread:6_NN1|)
(|det| |bread:6_NN1| |the:4_AT|)
(|ncmod| _ |bread:6_NN1| |fresh:5_JJ|)
(|det| |knife:2_NN1| |The:1_AT|)
```

The derived set of features includes the triples

{the:A:det←knife:N←cut:V:ncsubj,
A:det←knife:N←cut:V:ncsubj,
the:A:det←knife:N←V:ncsubj,
A:det←knife:N←V:ncsubj,
knife:N:ncsubj←cut:V→bread:N:dobj,
N:ncsubj←cut:V→bread:N:dobj,
knife:N:ncsubj←cut:V→N:dobj,
N:ncsubj←cut:V→N:dobj,...}

(The ← and → arrows indicate the direction of the head-modifier dependency)

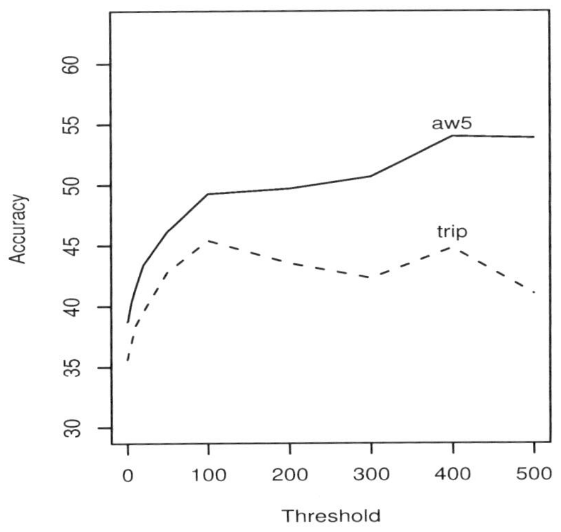

Figure 1: Effect of BNC frequency on test item accuracy for the **allwords5** and **triples** contexts

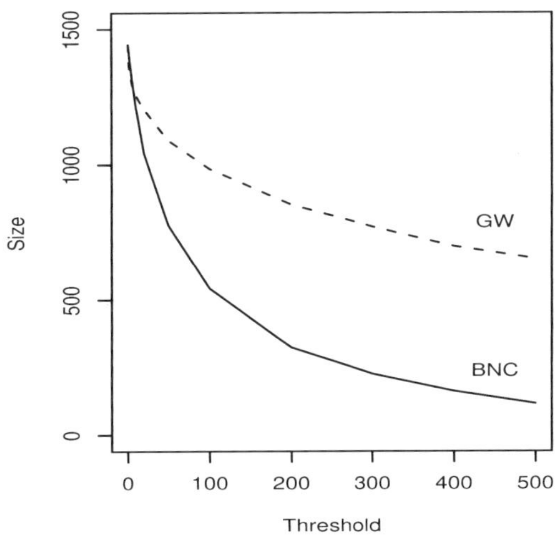

Figure 2: Effect of corpus frequency on dataset size for the BNC and Gigaword-derived corpus

Table 4 presents results for these contexts; in the case of parameterisable contexts the best-performing parameter setting is presented. We are currently unable to present results for the path-based contexts using the Gigaword corpus. It is clear from the accuracy figures that we have not matched the performance of the word similarity approach. The best-performing single context definition is **allwords** with a window parameter of 5, which yields accuracy of 38.74% (36.78% macro-average). We can combine the contributions of two contexts by generating a new kernel that is the sum of the linear kernels for the individual contexts;[6] the sum of **allwords5** and **triples** achieves the best performance with 42.34% (40.20% macro-average).

It might be expected that the richer context definitions provide sparser but more precise information, and that their relative performance might improve when only frequently observed word pairs are to be classified. However, thresholding inclusion in the test set on corpus frequency belies that expectation; as the threshold increases and the training data contains only more frequent pairs, all contexts show improved performance but the effect is strongest for the **allwords** and **midwords** contexts. Figure 1 shows threshold-accuracy curves for two representative contexts (the macro-accuracy curves are similar).

For all frequency thresholds above 6, the number of noun pairs with above-threshold corpus frequency is greater for the Gigaword corpus than for the BNC, and this effect is amplified with increasing threshold (see Figure 2). However, this difference in sparsity does not always induce an improvement in performance, but nor does the difference in corpus type consistently favour the BNC.

	BNC		Gigaword	
	Accuracy	Macro	Accuracy	Macro
aw	35.97%	33.39%	34.58%	32.62%
aw5	**38.74%**	**36.78%**	37.28%	35.25%
mw	32.29%	30.38%	36.24%	34.25%
agr	35.34%	33.40%	35.34%	33.34%
agr2	36.73%	34.81%	37.28%	35.59%
sp	33.54%	31.51%		
trip	35.62%	34.39%		
aw5+ trip	**42.34%**	**40.20%**		

Table 4: Classification results for relation similarity

[6]The summed kernel function value for a pair of items is simply the sum of the two kernel functions' values for the pair, i.e.:

$$K_{sum}(x, y) = K_1(\phi_1(x), \phi_1(y)) + K_2(\phi_2(x), \phi_2(y))$$

where ϕ_1, ϕ_2 are the context representations used by the two kernels. A detailed study of kernel combination is presented by Joachims et al. (2001).

6.2 String Kernels

The classification techniques described in the previous subsection represent the relational context for each word pair as a co-occurrence vector in an inner product space and compute the similarity between two pairs as a function of their vector representations. A different kind of similarity measure is provided by *string kernels*, which count the number of subsequences shared by two strings. This class of kernel function implicitly calculates an inner product in a feature space indexed by all possible subsequences (possibly restricted by length or contiguity), but the feature vectors are not explicitly represented. This approach affords our notion of context an increase in richness (features can be sequences of length ≥ 1) without incurring the computational cost of the exponential growth in the dimension of our feature space. A particularly flexible string kernel is the gap-weighted kernel described by Lodhi et al. (2002), which allows the subsequences to be non-contiguous but penalises the contribution of each subsequence to the kernel value according to the number of items occurring between the start and end of the subsequence, including those that do not belong to the subsequence (the "gaps").

The kernel is defined as follows. Let s and t be two strings of words belonging to a vocabulary Σ. A subsequence u of s is defined by a sequence of indices $\mathbf{i} = (i_1, \ldots, i_{|u|})$ such that $1 \leq i_1 < \ldots < i_{|u|} \leq |s|$, where s is the length of s. Let $l(\mathbf{i}) = i_{|u|} - i_1 + 1$ be the length of the subsequence in s. For example, if s is the string "cut the bread with the knife" and u is the subsequence "cut with" indexed by $\mathbf{i}$ then $l(\mathbf{i}) = 4$. λ is a decay parameter between 0 and 1. The gap-weighted kernel value for subsequences of length n of strings s and t is given by

$$K_{S_n}(s,t) = \sum_{u \in \Sigma^n} \sum_{\mathbf{i},\mathbf{j}:s[\mathbf{i}]=u=t[\mathbf{j}]} \lambda^{l(\mathbf{i})+l(\mathbf{j})}$$

Directly computing this function would be intractable, as the sum is over all $|\Sigma|^n$ possible subsequences of length n; however, Lodhi et al. (2002) present an efficient dynamic programming algorithm that can evaluate the kernel in $O(n|s||t|)$ time. Those authors' application of string kernels to text categorisation counts sequences of characters, but it is generally more suitable for NLP applications to use sequences of words (Cancedda et al., 2003).

This kernel calculates a similarity score for a pair of strings, but for context-based compound classification we are interested in the similarity between two *sets* of strings. We therefore define a *context kernel*, which sums the kernel scores for each pair of strings from the two context sets C_1, C_2 and normalises them by the number of pairs contributing to the sum:

$$K_{C_n}(C_1, C_2) = \frac{1}{|C_1||C_2|} \sum_{s \in C_1, t \in C_2} K_{S_n}(s,t)$$

That this is a valid kernel (i.e., defines an inner product in some induced vector space) can be proven using the definition of the *derived subsets kernel* in Shawe-Taylor and Cristianini (2004, p. 317). In our experiments we further normalise the kernel to ensure that $K_{C_n}(C_1, C_2) = 1$ if and only if $C_1 = C_2$.

To generate the context set for a given word pair, we extract a string from every sentence in the BNC where the pair of words occurs no more than eight words apart. On the hypothesis that the context between the target words was most important and to avoid the computational cost incurred by long strings, we only use this middle context. To facilitate generalisations over subsequences, the compound head is replaced by a marker HEAD and the modifier is replaced by a marker MOD. Word pairs for which no context strings were extracted (i.e., pairs which only occur as compounds in the corpus) are represented by a dummy string that matches no other. The value of λ is set to 0.5 as in Cancedda et al. (2003). Table 5 presents results for the context kernels with subsequence lengths 1,2,3 as well as the kernel sum of these three kernels. These kernels perform better than the relational vector space kernels, with the exception of the summed **allwords5 + triples** kernel.

7 Combining Contexts

We can use the method of kernel summation to combine information from different context types. If our intuition is correct that type and relation similarity provide different "views" of the same semantic relation, we would expect their combination to give better results than either taken alone. This is also suggested by the observation that the different context

	Accuracy	Macro
$n = 1$	15.94%	19.88%
$n = 2$	39.09%	37.23%
$n = 3$	39.29%	**39.29%**
$\Sigma_{1,2,3}$	**40.61%**	38.53%

Table 5: Classification results for gap-weighted string kernels with subsequence lengths 1,2,3 and the kernel sum of these kernels

	Accuracy	Macro
Rconj-G^2 + **aw5**	54.95%	53.50%
Rconj-G^2 + **triples**	56.20%	54.54%
Rconj-G^2 + **aw5** + **triples**	55.86%	54.13%
Rconj-G^2 + K_{C_2}	56.48%	54.89%
Rconj-G^2 + K_{C_Σ}	**56.55%**	**54.96%**

Table 6: Classification results for context combinations

types favour different relations: the summed string kernel is the best at identifying IN relations (70.45% precision, 46.67% recall), but Rconj-G^2 is best at identifying all others. This intuition is confirmed by our experiments, the results of which appear in Table 6. The best performance of 56.55% accuracy (54.96% macro-average) is attained by the combination of the G^2-transformed **Rconj** word similarity kernel and the summed string kernel K_{C_Σ}. We note that this result, using only information extracted from the BNC, compares favourably with the 56.76% accuracy (54.60% macro-average) results described by Ó Séaghdha (2007) for a WordNet-based method. The combination of **Rconj**-G^2 and **triples** is also competitive, demonstrating that a less flexible learning algorithm (the linear kernel) can perform well if it has access to a richer source of information (dependency paths).

8 Comparison with Prior Work

Previous work on compound semantics has tended to concentrate on either word or relation similarity. Approaches based on word similarity generally use information extracted from WordNet. For example, Girju et al. (2005) train SVM classifiers on hypernymy features for each constituent. Their best reported accuracy with an equivalent level of supervision to our work is 54.2%; they then improve performance by adding a significant amount of manually-annotated semantic information to the data, as does Girju (2006) in a multilingual context. It is difficult to make any conclusive comparison with these results due to fundamental differences in datasets and classification schemes.

Approaches based on relational similarity often use relative frequencies of fixed lexical sequences estimated from massive corpora. Lapata and Keller (2004) use Web counts for phrases *Noun P Noun* where *P* belongs to a predefined set of prepositions. This unsupervised approach gives state-of-the-art results on the assignment of prepositional paraphrases, but cannot be applied to deep semantic relations which cannot be directly identified in text. Turney and Littman (2005) search for phrases *Noun R Noun* where *R* is one of 64 "joining words". Turney (2006) presents a more flexible framework in which automatically identified n-gram features replace fixed unigrams and additional word pairs are generated by considering synonyms, but this method still requires a Web-magnitude corpus and a very large amount of computational time and storage space. The latter paper reports accuracy of 58.0% (55.9% macro-average), which remains the highest reported figure for corpus-based approaches and demonstrates that relational similarity can perform well given sufficient resources.

We are not aware of previous work that compares the effectiveness of different classes of context for compound interpretation, nor of work that investigates the utility of different corpora. We have also described the first application of string kernels to the compound task, though gap-weighted kernels have been used successfully for related tasks such as word sense disambiguation (Gliozzo et al., 2005) and relation extraction (Bunescu and Mooney, 2005).

9 Conclusion and Future Work

We have defined four kinds of co-occurrence contexts for compound interpretation and demonstrated that word similarity outperforms a range of relation contexts using information derived from the British National Corpus. Our experiments with the English Gigaword Corpus indicate that more data is not always better, and that large newswire corpora may not be ideally suited to general relation-based tasks.

On the other hand it might be expected to be very useful for disambiguating relations more typical of news stories (such as *tax cut*, *rail strike*).

Future research directions include developing more sophisticated context kernels. Cancedda et al. (2003) present a number of potentially useful refinements of the gap-weighted string kernel, including "soft matching" and differential values of λ for different words or word classes. We intend to combine the benefits of string kernels with the linguistic richness of syntactic parses by computing subsequence kernels on dependency paths. We have also begun to experiment with the tree kernels of Moschitti (2006), but are not yet in a position to report results. As mentioned in Section 2, we also intend to investigate the potential contribution of the sentential contexts that contain the compound tokens to be classified (token similarity).

While the BNC has many desirable properties, it may also be fruitful to investigate the utility of a large encyclopaedic corpus such as Wikipedia, which may be more explicit in its description of relations between real-world entities than typical text corpora. Wikipedia has shown promise as a resource for measuring word similarity (Strube and Ponzetto, 2006) and relation similarity (Suchanek et al. (2006)).

References

Ted Briscoe, John Carroll, and Rebecca Watson. 2006. The second release of the RASP system. In *Proceedings of the ACL-06 Interactive Presentation Sessions*.

Razvan C. Bunescu and Raymond J. Mooney. 2005. Subsequence kernels for relation extraction. In *Proceedings of the 19th Conference on Neural Information Processing Systems*.

Nicola Cancedda, Eric Gaussier, Cyril Goutte, and Jean-Michel Renders. 2003. Word-sequence kernels. *Journal of Machine Learning Research*, 3:1059–1082.

Chih-Chung Chang and Chih-Jen Lin, 2001. *LIBSVM: a library for support vector machines*. Software available at `http://www.csie.ntu.edu.tw/~cjlin/libsvm`.

Aron Culotta and Jeffrey Sorensen. 2004. Dependency tree kernels for relation extraction. In *Proceedings of ACL-04*.

Ted Dunning. 1993. Accurate methods for the statistics of surprise and coincidence. *Computational Linguistics*, 19(1):61–74.

Roxana Girju, Dan Moldovan, Marta Tatu, and Daniel Antohe. 2005. On the semantics of noun compounds. *Computer Speech and Language*, 19(4):479–496.

Roxana Girju. 2006. Out-of-context noun phrase semantic interpretation with cross-linguistic evidence. In *Proceedings of CIKM-06*.

Alfio Gliozzo, Claudio Giuliano, and Carlo Strapparava. 2005. Domain kernels for word sense disambiguation. In *Proceedings of ACL-05*.

David Graff, 2003. *English Gigaword*. Linguistic Data Consortium, Philadelphia.

Thorsten Joachims, Nello Cristianini, and John Shawe-Taylor. 2001. Composite kernels for hypertext categorisation. In *Proceedings of ICML-01*.

S. Sathiya Keerthi and Chih-Jen Lin. 2003. Asymptotic behaviors of support vector machines with Gaussian kernel. *Neural Computation*, 15:1667–1689.

Mirella Lapata and Frank Keller. 2004. The Web as a baseline: Evaluating the performance of unsupervised Web-based models for a range of NLP tasks. In *Proceedings of HLT-NAACL-04*.

Mark Lauer. 1995. *Designing Statistical Language Learners: Experiments on Compound Nouns*. Ph.D. thesis, Macquarie University.

Huma Lodhi, Craig Saunders, John Shawe-Taylor, Nello Cristianini, and Chris Watkins. 2002. Text classification using string kernels. *Journal of Machine Learning Research*, 2:419–444.

Alessandro Moschitti. 2006. Efficient convolution kernels for dependency and constituent syntactic trees. In *Proceedings of ECML-06*.

Sebastian Padó and Mirella Lapata. 2003. Constructing semantic space models from parsed corpora. In *Proceedings of ACL-03*.

Diarmuid Ó Séaghdha. 2007. Annotating and learning compound noun semantics. In *Proceedings of the ACL-07 Student Research Workshop*.

John Shawe-Taylor and Nello Cristianini. 2004. *Kernel Methods for Pattern Analysis*. Cambridge University Press, Cambridge.

Michael Strube and Simone Paolo Ponzetto. 2006. WikiRelate! computing semantic relatedness using Wikipedia. In *Proceedings of AAAI-06*.

Fabian M. Suchanek, Georgiana Ifrim, and Gerhard Weikum. 2006. LEILA: Learning to extract information by linguistic analysis. In *Proceedings of the ACL-06 Workshop on Ontology Learning and Population*.

Peter D. Turney and Michael L. Littman. 2005. Corpus-based learning of analogies and semantic relations. *Machine Learning*, 60(1–3):251–278.

Peter D. Turney. 2006. Similarity of semantic relations. *Computational Linguistics*, 32(3):379–416.

Learning Dependency Relations of Japanese Compound Functional Expressions

Takehito Utsuro[†] and **Takao Shime**[‡] and **Masatoshi Tsuchiya**[††]
Suguru Matsuyoshi[†‡] and **Satoshi Sato**[†‡]
†Graduate School of Systems and Information Engineering, University of Tsukuba,
1-1-1, Tennodai, Tsukuba, 305-8573, JAPAN
‡NEC Corporation
††Computer Center, Toyohashi University of Technology,
Tenpaku-cho, Toyohashi, 441–8580, JAPAN
†‡Graduate School of Engineering, Nagoya University,
Furo-cho, Chikusa-ku, Nagoya, 464–8603, JAPAN

Abstract

This paper proposes an approach of processing Japanese compound functional expressions by identifying them and analyzing their dependency relations through a machine learning technique. First, we formalize the task of identifying Japanese compound functional expressions in a text as a machine learning based chunking problem. Next, against the results of identifying compound functional expressions, we apply the method of dependency analysis based on the cascaded chunking model. The results of experimental evaluation show that, the dependency analysis model achieves improvements when applied after identifying compound functional expressions, compared with the case where it is applied without identifying compound functional expressions.

1 Introduction

In addition to single functional words, the Japanese language has many more compound functional expressions which consist of more than one word including both content words and functional words. They are very important for recognizing syntactic structures of Japanese sentences and for understanding their semantic content. Recognition and understanding of them are also very important for various kinds of NLP applications such as dialogue systems, machine translation, and question answering. However, recognition and semantic interpretation of compound functional expressions are especially difficult because it often happens that one compound expression may have both a literal (i.e. compositional) *content word* usage and a non-literal (i.e. non-compositional) *functional* usage.

For example, Table 1 shows two example sentences of a compound expression "に (ni) ついて (tsuite)", which consists of a post-positional particle "に (ni)", and a conjugated form "ついて (tsuite)" of a verb "つく (tsuku)". In the sentence (A), the compound expression functions as a case-marking particle and has a non-compositional functional meaning "*about*". On the other hand, in the sentence (B), the expression simply corresponds to a literal concatenation of the usages of the constituents: the post-positional particle "に (ni)" and the verb "ついて (tsuite)", and has a content word meaning "*follow*". Therefore, when considering machine translation of these Japanese sentences into English, it is necessary to judge precisely the usage of the compound expression "に (ni) ついて (tsuite)", as shown in the English translation of the two sentences in Table 1.

There exist widely-used Japanese text processing tools, i.e. combinations of a morphological analysis tool and a subsequent parsing tool, such as JUMAN[1]+ KNP[2] and ChaSen[3]+ CaboCha[4]. However, they process those compound expressions only partially, in that their morphological analysis dictionaries list only a limited number of compound expressions. Furthermore, even if certain expressions are listed in a morphological analysis dictionary, those existing tools often fail in resolving the ambigui-

[1]http://nlp.kuee.kyoto-u.ac.jp/nl-resource/juman-e.html
[2]http://nlp.kuee.kyoto-u.ac.jp/nl-resource/knp-e.html
[3]http://chasen.naist.jp/hiki/ChaSen/
[4]http://chasen.org/~taku/software/cabocha/

Proceedings of the Workshop on A Broader Perspective on Multiword Expressions, pages 65–72,
Prague, June 2007.

(A)	私 (watashi) (*I*)	は (ha) (*TOP*)	彼 (kare) (*he*)	に (ni) ついて (tsuite) (*about*)		話した (hanashita) (*talked*)
	(I talked about him.)					
(B)	私 (watashi) (*I*)	は (ha) (*TOP*)	彼 (kare) (*he*)	に (ni) (*ACC*)	ついて (tsuite) (*follow*)	走った (hashitta) (*ran*)
	(I ran following him.)					

Table 1: Translation Selection of a Japanese Compound Expression "に (ni) ついて (tsuite)"

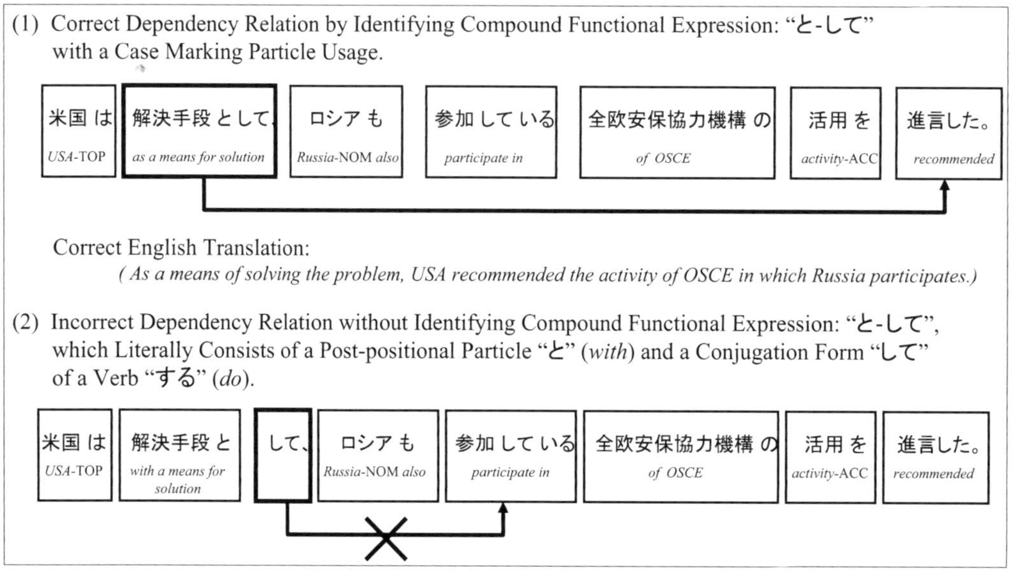

Figure 1: Example of Improving Dependency Analysis of Compound Functional Expressions by Identifying them before Dependency Analysis

ties of their usages, such as those in Table 1. This is mainly because the framework of these existing tools is not designed so as to resolve such ambiguities of compound (possibly functional) expressions by carefully considering the context of those expressions.

Actually, as we introduce in the next section, as a first step towards studying computational processing of compound functional expressions, we start with 125 major functional expressions which have non-compositional usages, as well as their variants (337 expressions in total). Out of those 337 expressions, 111 have both a *content word* usage and a *functional* usage. However, the combination of JUMAN+KNP is capable of distinguishing the two usages only for 43 of the 111 expressions, and the combination of ChaSen+CaboCha only for 40 of those 111 expressions. Furthermore, the failure in distinguishing the two usages may cause errors of syntactic analysis. For example, (1) of Figure 1 gives an example of identifying a correct modifiee of the second *bunsetsu* segment [5] "解決手段として (*as a means for solution*)" including a Japanese compound functional expression "として (*as*)", by appropriately detecting the compound functional expression before dependency analysis. On the other hand, (2) of Figure 1 gives an example of incorrectly indicating an erroneous modifiee of the third bunsetsu "して", which actually happens if we do not identify the compound functional expression "として (*as*)" before dependency analysis of this sentence.

Considering such a situation, it is necessary to develop a tool which properly recognizes and semantically interprets Japanese compound functional expressions. This paper proposes an approach of processing Japanese compound functional expressions by identifying them and analyzing their dependency relations through a machine learning technique. The overall flow of processing compound functional expressions in a Japanese sentence is il-

[5] A Japanese *bunsetsu* segment is a phrasal unit which consists of at least one content word and zero or more functional words.

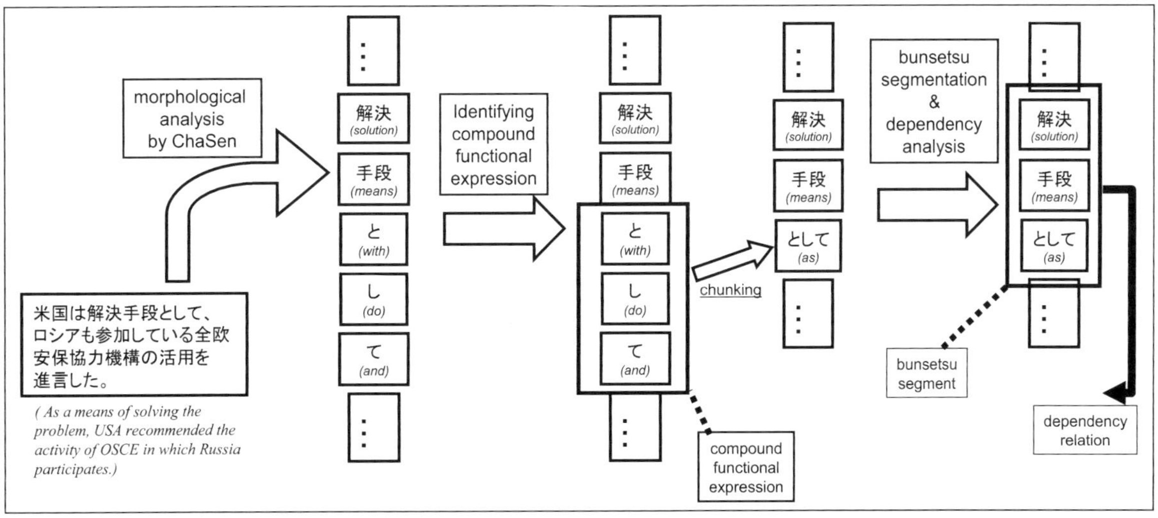

Figure 2: Overall Flow of Processing Compound Functional Expressions in a Japanese Sentence

lustrated in Figure 2. First of all, we assume a sequence of morphemes obtained by a variant of ChaSen with all the compound functional expressions removed from its outputs, as an input to our procedure of identifying compound functional expressions and analyzing their dependency relations. We formalize the task of identifying Japanese compound functional expressions in a text as a machine learning based chunking problem (Tsuchiya et al., 2006). We employ the technique of Support Vector Machines (SVMs) (Vapnik, 1998) as the machine learning technique, which has been successfully applied to various natural language processing tasks including chunking tasks such as phrase chunking and named entity chunking. Next, against the results of identifying compound functional expressions, we apply the method of dependency analysis based on the cascaded chunking model (Kudo and Matsumoto, 2002), which is simple and efficient because it parses a sentence deterministically only deciding whether the current bunsetsu segment modifies the one on its immediate right hand side. As we showed in Figure 1, identifying compound functional expressions before analyzing dependencies in a sentence does actually help deciding dependency relations of compound functional expressions.

In the experimental evaluation, we focus on 59 expressions having balanced distribution of their usages in the newspaper text corpus and are among the most difficult ones in terms of their identification in a text. We first show that the proposed method of chunking compound functional expressions significantly outperforms existing Japanese text processing tools. Next, we further show that the dependency analysis model of (Kudo and Matsumoto, 2002) applied to the results of identifying compound functional expressions significantly outperforms the one applied to the results without identifying compound functional expressions.

2 Japanese Compound Functional Expressions

There exist several collections which list Japanese functional expressions and examine their usages. For example, (Morita and Matsuki, 1989) examine 450 functional expressions and (Group Jamashii, 1998) also lists 965 expressions and their example sentences. Compared with those two collections, *Gendaigo Hukugouji Youreishu* (National Language Research Institute, 2001) (henceforth, denoted as *GHY*) concentrates on 125 major functional expressions which have non-compositional usages, as well as their variants[6], and collects example sentences of those expressions. As we mentioned in the previous section, as a first step towards developing a tool for identifying Japanese compound functional expressions, we start with those 125 major functional expressions and their variants (337 expressions in to-

[6]For each of those 125 major expressions, the differences between it and its variants are summarized as below: i) insertion/deletion/alternation of certain particles, ii) alternation of synonymous words, iii) normal/honorific/conversational forms, iv) base/adnominal/negative forms.

(a) Classification of Compound Functional Expressions based on Grammatical Function

Grammatical Function Type		# of major expressions	# of variants	Example
post-positional particle type	conjunctive particle	36	67	くせに (kuse-ni)
	case-marking particle	45	121	として (to-shite)
	adnominal particle	2	3	という (to-iu)
auxiliary verb type		42	146	ていい (te-ii)
total		125	337	—

(b) Examples of Classifying Functional/Content Usages

	Expression	Example sentence (English translation)	Usage
(1)	くせに (kuse-ni)	兄には金をやる[くせに]、おれには手紙をよこしただけだ。 (To my brother, (someone) gave money, *while* (he/she) did nothing to me but just sent a letter.)	functional (くせに (kuse-ni) = *while*)
(2)	くせに (kuse-ni)	彼のその[くせに]みんな驚いた。 (They all were surprised *by* his *habit*.)	content (∼ くせに (kuse-ni) = *by one's habit*
(3)	として (to-shite)	彼はその問題の専門家[として]知られている。 (He is known *as* an expert of the problem.)	functional (∼ として (to-shite) = *as* ∼)
(4)	として (to-shite)	これが正しいかどうかはっきり[として]下さい。 (Please *make* it clear whether this is true or not.)	content (∼ を ∼ として (to-shite) = *make* ∼ ∼
(5)	という (to-iu)	彼は生きている[という]知らせを聞いた。 (I heard *that* he is alive.)	functional (∼ という (to-iu) = *that* ∼)
(6)	という (to-iu)	「遊びに来て下さい」[という]人もいる。 (Somebody *says* "Please visit us.".)	content (∼ という (to-iu) = *say (that)* ∼)
(7)	ていい (te-ii)	この議論が終ったら休憩し[ていい]。 (You *may* have a break after we finish this discussion.)	functional (∼ ていい (te-ii) = *may* ∼)
(8)	ていい (te-ii)	このかばんは大きく[ていい]。 (This bag is *nice because* it is big.)	content (∼ ていい (te-ii) = *nice because* ∼)

Table 2: Classification and Example Usages of Compound Functional Expressions

tal). In this paper, following (Sag et al., 2002), we regard each variant as a fixed expression, rather than a semi-fixed expression or a syntactically-flexible expression [7]. Then, we focus on evaluating the effectiveness of straightforwardly applying a standard chunking technique to the task of identifying Japanese compound functional expressions.

As in Table 2 (a), according to their grammatical functions, those 337 expressions in total are roughly classified into *post-positional particle* type, and *auxiliary verb* type. Functional expressions of post-positional particle type are further classified into three subtypes: i) conjunctive particle types, which are used for constructing subordinate clauses, ii) case-marking particle types, iii) adnominal particle types, which are used for constructing adnominal clauses. Furthermore, for examples of compound functional expressions listed in Table 2 (a), Table 2 (b) gives their example sentences as well as the description of their usages.

3 Identifying Compound Functional Expressions by Chunking with SVMs

This section describes summaries of formalizing the chunking task using SVMs (Tsuchiya et al., 2006). In this paper, we use an SVMs-based chunking tool YamCha[8] (Kudo and Matsumoto, 2001). In the SVMs-based chunking framework, SVMs are used as classifiers for assigning labels for representing chunks to each token. In our task of chunking Japanese compound functional expressions, each

[7] Compound functional expressions of auxiliary verb types can be regarded as syntactically-flexible expressions.

[8] `http://chasen.org/~taku/software/yamcha/`

sentence is represented as a sequence of morphemes, where a morpheme is regarded as a token.

3.1 Chunk Representation

For representing proper chunks, we employ IOB2 representation, which has been studied well in various chunking tasks of natural language processing. This method uses the following set of three labels for representing proper chunks.

- **I** Current token is a middle or the end of a chunk consisting of more than one token.
- **O** Current token is outside of any chunk.
- **B** Current token is the beginning of a chunk.

Given a candidate expression, we classify the usages of the expression into two classes: *functional* and *content*. Accordingly, we distinguish the chunks of the two types: the *functional* type chunk and the *content* type chunk. In total, we have the following five labels for representing those chunks: **B-functional, I-functional, B-content, I-content**, and **O**. Finally, as for extending SVMs to multi-class classifiers, we experimentally compare the *pairwise* method and the *one vs. rest* method, where the *pairwise* method slightly outperformed the *one vs. rest* method. Throughout the paper, we show results with the *pairwise* method.

3.2 Features

For the feature sets for training/testing of SVMs, we use the information available in the surrounding context, such as the morphemes, their parts-of-speech tags, as well as the chunk labels. More precisely, suppose that we identify the chunk label c_i for the i-th morpheme:

	$\longrightarrow$ Parsing Direction $\longrightarrow$				
Morpheme	m_{i-2}	m_{i-1}	m_i	m_{i+1}	m_{i+2}
Feature set at a position	F_{i-2}	F_{i-1}	F_i	F_{i+1}	F_{i+2}
Chunk label	c_{i-2}	c_{i-1}	$\boxed{c_i}$		

Here, m_i is the morpheme appearing at i-th position, F_i is the feature set at i-th position, and c_i is the chunk label for i-th morpheme. Roughly speaking, when identifying the chunk label c_i for the i-th morpheme, we use the feature sets F_{i-2}, F_{i-1}, F_i, F_{i+1}, F_{i+2} at the positions $i-2$, $i-1$, i, $i+1$, $i+2$, as well as the preceding two chunk labels c_{i-2} and c_{i-1}. The detailed definition of the feature set F_i at i-th position is given in (Tsuchiya et al., 2006), which mainly consists of morphemes as well as information on the candidate compound functional expression at i-th position.

4 Learning Dependency Relations of Japanese Compound Functional Expressions

4.1 Japanese Dependency Analysis using Cascaded Chunking

4.1.1 Cascaded Chunking Model

First of all, we define a Japanese sentence as a sequence of bunsetsu segments $B = \langle b_1, b_2, \ldots, b_m \rangle$ and its syntactic structure as a sequence of dependency patterns $D = \langle Dep(1), Dep(2), \ldots, Dep(m-1) \rangle$, where $Dep(i) = j$ means that the bunsetsu segment b_i depends on (modifies) bunsetsu segment b_j. In this framework, we assume that the dependency sequence D satisfies the following two constraints:

1. Japanese is a head-final language. Thus, except for the rightmost one, each bunsetsu segment modifies exactly one bunsetsu segment among those appearing to its right.
2. Dependencies do not cross one another.

Unlike probabilistic dependency analysis models of Japanese, the cascaded chunking model of Kudo and Matsumoto (2002) does not require the probabilities of dependencies and parses a sentence deterministically. Since Japanese is a head-final language, and the chunking can be regarded as the creation of a dependency between two bunsetsu segments, this model simplifies the process of Japanese dependency analysis as follows:[9]

1. Put an **O** tag on all bunsetsu segments. The **O** tag indicates that the dependency relation of the current segment is undecided.
2. For each bunsetsu segment with an **O** tag, decide whether it modifies the bunsetsu segment on its immediate right hand side. If so, the **O** tag is replaced with a **D** tag.
3. Delete all bunsetsu segments with a **D** tag that immediately follows a bunsetsu segment with an **O** tag.

[9]The **O** and **D** tags used in this section have no relation to those chunk reppresentation tags introduced in section 3.1.

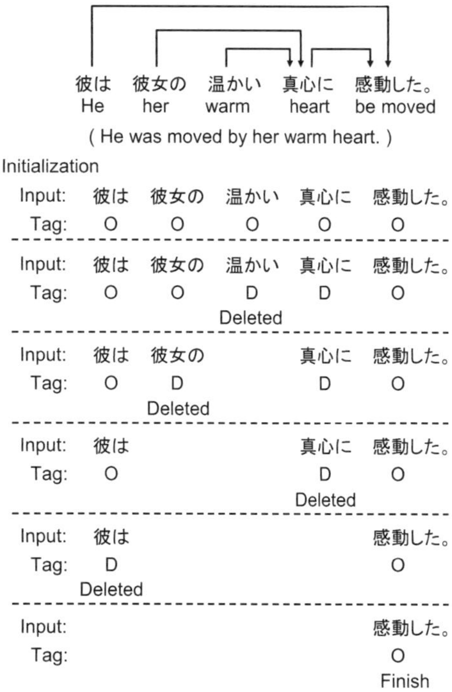

Figure 3: Example of the Parsing Process with Cascaded Chunking Model

4. Terminate the algorithm if a single bunsetsu segment remains, otherwise return to the step 2 and repeat.

Figure 3 shows an example of the parsing process with the cascaded chunking model.

4.1.2 Features

As a Japanese dependency analyzer based on the cascaded chunking model, we use the publicly available version of CaboCha (Kudo and Matsumoto, 2002), which is trained with the manually parsed sentences of Kyoto text corpus (Kurohashi and Nagao, 1998), that are 38,400 sentences selected from the 1995 Mainichi newspaper text.

The standard feature set used by CaboCha consists of **static features** and **dynamic features**. Static features are those solely defined once the pair of modifier/modifiee bunsetsu segments is specified. For the pair of modifier/modifiee bunsetsu segments, the following are used as static features: head words and their parts-of-speech tags, inflection-types/forms, functional words and their parts-of-speech tags, inflection-types/forms, inflection forms of the words that appear at the end of bunsetsu segments. As for features between modifier/modifiee bunsetsu segments, the distance of modifier/modifiee bunsetsu segments, existence of case-particles, brackets, quotation-marks, and punctuation-marks are used as static features. On the other hand, dynamic features are created during the parsing process, so that, when a certain dependency relation is determined, it can have some influence on other dependency relations. Dynamic features include bunsetsu segments modifying the current candidate modifiee (see Kudo and Matsumoto (2002) for the details).

4.2 Coping with Compound Functional Expressions

As we show in Figure 2, a compound functional expression is identified as a sequence of several morphemes and then chunked into one morpheme. The result of this identification process is then transformed into the sequence of bunsetsu segments. Finally, to this modified sequence of bunsetsu segments, the method of dependency analysis based on the cascaded chunking model is applied.

Here, when chunking a sequence of several morphemes constituting a compound functional expression, the following two cases may exist:

(A) As in the case of the example (A) in Table 1, the two morphemes constituting a compound functional expression "に (ni) ついて (tsuite)" overlaps the boundary of two bunsetsu segments. In such a case, when chunking the two morphemes into one morpheme corresponding to a compound functional expression, those two bunsetsu segments are concatenated into one bunsetsu segment.

彼 に kare ni *(he)*	ついて tsuite	⟹	彼 について kare ni-tsuite *(he)* *(about)*

(B) As we show below, a compound functional expression "こと (koto) が (ga) ある (aru)" overlaps the boundary of two bunsetsu segments, though the two bunsetsu segments concatenating into one bunsetsu segment does include no content words. In such a case, its immediate left bunsetsu segment ("行っ (itt) た (ta)" in the example below), which corresponds to the content word part of "こと (koto) が (ga) ある (aru)", has to be concatenated into the bunsetsu segment "こと (koto) が (ga) ある (aru)".

行っ た itt ta *(went)*	こと が koto ga	ある aru	⟹	行っ た ことがある itt ta koto-ga-aru *(have been ∼)*

Next, to the compound functional expression, we assign one of the four grammatical function types listed in Table 2 as its POS tag. For example, the compound functional expression "に (ni) ついて (tsuite)" in (A) above is assigned the grammatical function type "case-marking particle type", while "こと (koto) が (ga) ある (aru)" in (B) is assigned "auxiliary verb type".

These modifications cause differences in the final feature representations. For example, let us compare the feature representations of the modifier bunsetsu segments in (1) and (2) of Figure 1. In (1), the modifier bunsetsu segment is "解決手段として" which has the compound functional expression "として" in its functional word part. On the other hand, in (2), the modifier bunsetsu segment is "して", which corresponds to the literal verb usage of a part of the compound functional expression "として". In the final feature representations below, this causes the following differences in head words and functional words / POS of the modifier bunsetsu segments:

	(1) of Figure 1	(2) of Figure 1
head word	手段 *(means)*	する *(do)*
functional word POS	として *(as)* subsequent to nominal / modifying predicate	て *(and)* conjunctive particle

5 Experimental Evaluation

5.1 Training/Test Data Sets

For the training of chunking compound functional expressions, we collected 2,429 example sentences from the 1995 Mainichi newspaper text corpus. For each of the 59 compound functional expressions for evaluation mentioned in section 1, at least 50 examples are included in this training set. For the testing of chunking compound functional expressions, as well as training/testing of learning dependencies of compound functional expressions, we used manually-parsed sentences of Kyoto text corpus (Kurohashi and Nagao, 1998), that are 38,400 sentences selected from the 1995 Mainichi newspaper text (the 2,429 sentences above are selected so that they are exclusive of the 37,400 sentences of Kyoto text corpus.). To those data sets, we manually annotate usage labels of the 59 compound functional expressions (details in Table 3).

	Usages			# of sentences
	functional	content	total	
for chunker training	1918	1165	3083	2429
Kyoto text corpus	5744	1959	7703	38400

Table 3: Statistics of Data Sets

	Identifying *functional* chunks			Acc. of classifying *functional / content* chunks
	Prec.	Rec.	$F_{\beta=1}$	
majority (= *functional*)	74.6	100	85.5	74.6
Juman/KNP	85.8	40.5	55.0	58.4
ChaSen/CaboCha	85.2	26.7	40.6	51.1
SVM	91.4	94.6	**92.9**	**89.3**

Table 4: Evaluation Results of Chunking (%)

5.2 Chunking

As we show in Table 4, performance of our SVMs-based chunkers as well as several baselines including existing Japanese text processing tools is evaluated in terms of precision/recall/$F_{\beta=1}$ of identifying all the 5,744 *functional* chunks included in the test data (Kyoto text corpus in Table 3). Performance is evaluated also in terms of accuracy of classifying detected candidate expressions into *functional/content* chunks. Among those baselines, "majority (= *functional*)" always assigns *functional* usage to the detected candidate expressions. Performance of our SVMs-based chunkers is measured through 10-fold cross validation. Our SVMs-based chunker significantly outperforms those baselines both in $F_{\beta=1}$ and classification accuracy. As we mentioned in section 1, existing Japanese text processing tools process compound functional expressions only partially, which causes damage in recall in Table 4.

5.3 Analyzing Dependency Relations

We evaluate the accuracies of judging dependency relations of compound functional expressions by the variant of CaboCha trained with Kyoto text corpus annotated with usage labels of compound functional expressions. This performance is measured through 10-fold cross validation with the modified version of the Kyoto text corpus. In the evaluation phase, according to the flow of Figure 2, first we apply the chunker of compound functional expressions trained with all the 2,429 sentences in Table 3 and obtain the results of chunked compound functional expressions with about 90% correct rate. Then, bunsetsu segmentation and dependency analysis are per-

		modifier	modifiee
baselines	CaboCha (w/o FE)	72.5	**88.0**
	CaboCha (public)	73.9	87.6
chunker + CaboCha (proposed)		**74.0**	**88.0**
reference + CaboCha (proposed)		74.4	88.1

Table 5: Accuracies of Identifying Modifier(s)/Modifiee (%)

formed by our variant of CaboCha, where accuracies of identifying modifier(s)/modifiee of compound functional expressions are measured as in Table 5 ("chunker + CaboCha (proposed)" denotes that inputs to CaboCha (proposed) are with 90% correct rate, while "reference + CaboCha (proposed)" denotes that they are with 100% correct rate). Here, "CaboCha (w/o FE)" denotes a baseline variant of CaboCha, with all the compound functional expressions removed from its inputs (which are outputs from ChaSen), while "CaoboCha (public)" denotes the publicly available version of CaboCha, which have some portion of the compound functional expressions included in its inputs.

For the modifier accuracy, the difference of "chunker + CaboCha (proposed)" and "CaboCha (w/o FE)" is statistically significant at a level of 0.05. Identifying compound functional expressions typically contributes to improvements when the literal constituents of a compound functional expression include a verb. In such a case, for bunsetsu segments which usually modifies a verb, an incorrect modifee candidate is removed, which results in improvements in the modifier accuracy. The difference between 'CaoboCha (public)" and "chunker + CaboCha (proposed)" is slight because the publicly available version of CaboCha seems to include compound functional expressions which are damaged in identifying their modifiers with "CaboCha (w/o FE)". For the modifiee accuracy, the difference of "chunker + CaboCha (proposed)" and "CaboCha (w/o FE)" is zero. Here, more than 100 instances of improvements like the one in Figure 1 are observed, while almost the same number of additional failures are also observed mainly because of the sparseness problem. Furthermore, in the case of the modifiee accuracy, it is somehow difficult to expect improvement because identifying modifiees of *functional/content* bunsetsu segments mostly depends on features other than *functional/content* distinction.

6 Concluding Remarks

We proposed an approach of processing Japanese compound functional expressions by identifying them and analyzing their dependency relations through a machine learning technique. This approach is novel in that it has never been applied to any language so far. Experimental evaluation showed that the dependency analysis model applied to the results of identifying compound functional expressions significantly outperforms the one applied to the results without identifying compound functional expressions. The proposed framework has advantages over an approach based on manually created rules such as the one in (Shudo et al., 2004), in that it requires human cost to create manually and maintain those rules. Related works include Nivre and Nilsson (2004), which reports improvement of Swedish parsing when multi word units are manually annotated.

References

Group Jamashii, editor. 1998. *Nihongo Bunkei Jiten*. Kuroshio Publisher. (in Japanese).

T. Kudo and Y. Matsumoto. 2001. Chunking with support vector machines. In *Proc. 2nd NAACL*, pages 192–199.

T. Kudo and Y. Matsumoto. 2002. Japanese dependency analyisis using cascaded chunking. In *Proc. 6th CoNLL*, pages 63–69.

S. Kurohashi and M. Nagao. 1998. Building a Japanese parsed corpus while improving the parsing system. In *Proc. 1st LREC*, pages 719–724.

Y. Morita and M. Matsuki. 1989. *Nihongo Hyougen Bunkei*, volume 5 of *NAFL Sensho*. ALC. (in Japanese).

National Language Research Institute. 2001. *Gendaigo Hukugouji Youreishu*. (in Japanese).

J. Nivre and J. Nilsson. 2004. Multiword units in syntactic parsing. In *Proc. LREC Workshop, Methodologies and Evaluation of Multiword Units in Real-World Applications*, pages 39–46.

I. Sag, T. Baldwin, F. Bond, A. Copestake, and D. Flickinger. 2002. Multiword expressions: A pain in the neck for NLP. In *Proc. 3rd CICLING*, pages 1–15.

K. Shudo, T. Tanabe, M. Takahashi, and K. Yoshimura. 2004. MWEs as non-propositional content indicators. In *Proc. 2nd ACL Workshop on Multiword Expressions: Integrating Processing*, pages 32–39.

M. Tsuchiya, T. Shime, T. Takagi, T. Utsuro, K. Uchimoto, S. Matsuyoshi, S. Sato, and S. Nakagawa. 2006. Chunking Japanese compound functional expressions by machine learning. In *Proc. Workshop on Multi-Word-Expressions in a Multilingual Context*, pages 25–32.

V. N. Vapnik. 1998. *Statistical Learning Theory*. Wiley-Interscience.

Semantic Labeling of Compound Nominalization in Chinese

Jinglei Zhao, Hui Liu & Ruzhan Lu
Department of Computer Science
Shanghai Jiao Tong University
800 Dongchuan Road Shanghai, China
{zjl,lh_charles,rzlu}@sjtu.edu.cn

Abstract

This paper discusses the semantic interpretation of compound nominalizations in Chinese. We propose four coarse-grained semantic roles of the noun modifier and use a Maximum Entropy Model to label such relations in a compound nominalization. The feature functions used for the model are web-based statistics acquired via role related paraphrase patterns, which are formed by a set of word instances of prepositions, support verbs, feature nouns and aspect markers. By applying a sub-linear transformation and discretization of the raw statistics, a rate of approximately 77% is obtained for classification of the four semantic relations.

1 Introduction

A nominal compound (NC) is the concatenation of any two or more nominal concepts which functions as a third nominal concept (Finin, 1980). (Leonard, 1984) observed that the amount of NCs had been increasing explosively in English in recent years. NCs such as *satellite navigation system* are abundant in news and technical texts. In other languages such as Chinese, NCs have been more productive since earlier days as evidenced by the fact that many simple words in Chinese are actually a result of compounding of morphemes.

Many aspects in Natural Language Processing (NLP), such as machine translation, information retrieval, question answering, etc. call for the automatic interpretation of NCs, that is, making explicit the underlying semantic relationships between the constituent concepts. For example, the semantic relations involved in *satellite communication system* can be expressed by the conceptual graph (Sowa, 1984) in Figure 1, in which, for instance, the semantic relation between *satellite* and *communication* is MANNER. Due to the productivity of NCs and the lack of syntactic clues to guide the interpretation process, the automatic interpretation of NCs has been proven to be a very difficult problem in NLP.

In this paper, we deal with the semantic interpretation of NCs in Chinese. Especially, we will focus on a subset of NCs in which the head word is a verb nominalization. Nominalization is a common phenomenon across languages in which a predicative expression is transformed to refer to an event or a property. For example, the English verb *communicate* has the related nominalized form *communication*. Different from English, Chinese has little morphology. Verb nominalization in Chinese has the same form as the verb predicate.

Nominalizations retain the argument structure of the corresponding predicates. The semantic relation between a noun modifier and a verb nominalization head can be characterized by the semantic role the modifier can take respecting to the corresponding verb predicate. Our method uses a Maximum Entropy model to label coarse-grained semantic roles in Chinese compound nominalizations. Unlike most approaches in compound interpretation and semantic role labeling, we don't exploit features from any parsed texts or lexical knowledge sources. Instead, features are acquired using web-based statis-

Proceedings of the Workshop on A Broader Perspective on Multiword Expressions, pages 73–80,
Prague, June 2007.

[satellite]←(MANNER)←[communication]←(TELIC)←[system]

Figure 1: The conceptual graph for *satellite communication system*

tics (PMI-IR) produced from paraphrase patterns of the compound Nominalization.

The remainder of the paper is organized as follows: Section 2 describes related works. Section 3 describes the semantic relations for our labeling task. Section 4 introduces the paraphrase patterns used. Section 5 gives a detailed description of our algorithm. Section 6 presents the experimental result. Finally, in Section 7, we give the conclusions and discuss future work.

2 Related Works

2.1 Nominal Compound Interpretation

The methods used in the semantic interpretation of NCs fall into two main categories: rule-based ones and statistic-based ones. The rule-based approaches such as (Finin, 1980; Mcdonald, 1982; Leonard, 1984; Vanderwende, 1995) think that the interpretation of NCs depends heavily on the constituent concepts and model the semantic interpretation as a slot-filling process. Various rules are employed by such approaches to determine, for example, whether the modifier can fill in one slot of the head.

The statistic-based approaches view the semantic interpretation as a multi-class classification problem. (Rosario and Hearst, 2001; Moldovan et al., 2004; Kim and Baldwin, 2005) use supervised methods and explore classification features from a simple structured type hierarchy. (Kim and Baldwin, 2006) use a set of seed verbs to characterize the semantic relation between the constituent nouns and explores a parsed corpus to classify NCs. (Turney, 2005) uses latent relational analysis to classify NCs. The similarity between two NCs is characterized by the similarity between their related pattern set.

(Lauer, 1995) is the first to use paraphrase based unsupervised statistical models to classify semantic relations of NCs. (Lapata, 2000; Grover et al., 2005; Nicholson, 2005) use paraphrase statistics computed from parsed texts to interpret compound nominalization, but the relations used are purely syntactic. Lapata(2000) only classifies syntactic relations of subject and object. Grover(2005) and Nicholson (2005) classify relations of subject, object and prepositional object.

2.2 Semantic Role Labeling of Nominalization

Most previous work on semantic role labeling of nominalizations are conducted in the situation where a verb nominalization is the head of a general noun phrase. (Dahl et al., 1987; Hull and Gomez, 1996) use hand-coded slot-filling rules to determine the semantic roles of the arguments of a nominalization. In such approaches, first, parsers are used to identify syntactic clues such as prepositional types. Then, rules are applied to label semantic roles according to clues and constraints of different roles.

Supervised machine learning methods become prevalent in recent years in semantic role labeling of verb nominalizations as part of the resurgence of research in shallow semantic analysis. (Pradhan et al., 2004) use a SVM classifier for the semantic role labeling of nominalizations in English and Chinese based on the FrameNet database and the Chinese PropBank respectively. (Xue, 2006) uses the Chinese Nombank to label nominalizations in Chinese. Compared to English, the main difficulty of using supervised method for Chinese, as noted by Xue (2006), is that the precision of current parsers of Chinese is very low due to the lack of morphology, difficulty in segmentation and lack of sufficient training materials in Chinese.

2.3 Web as a large Corpus

Data sparseness is the most notorious hinder for applying statistical methods in natural language processing. However, the World Wide Web can be seen as a large corpus. (Grefenstette and Nioche, 2000; Jones and Ghani, 2000) use the web to generate corpora for languages for which electronic resources are scarce. (Zhu and Rosenfeld, 2001) use Web-based n-gram counts for language modeling. (Keller and Lapata, 2003) show that Web page counts and n-gram frequency counts are highly correlated in a log scale.

3 Semantic Relations

Although verb nominalization is commonly considered to have arguments as the verb predicate, Xue(2006) finds that there tend to be fewer arguments and fewer types of adjuncts in verb nominalizations compared to verb predicates in Chinese. We argue that this phenomenon is more obvious in compound nominalization. By analyzing a set of compound nominalizations of length two from a balanced corpus(Jin et al., 2003), we find the semantic relations between a noun modifier and a verb nominalization head can be characterized by four coarse-grained semantic roles: Proto-Agent (PA), Proto-Patient (PP), Range (RA) and Manner (MA). This is illustrated by Table1.

Relations	Examples	
PA	血液 循环	(Blood Circulation)
	鸟类 迁徙	(Bird Migration)
PP	企业 管理	(Enterprise Management)
	动物 分类	(Animal Categorization)
MA	激光 存储	(Laser Storage)
	卫星 通信	(Satellite Communication)
RA	全球 定位	(Global Positioning)
	长期 发展	(Long-time Development)

Table 1: Semantic Relations between Noun Modifier and Verb Nominalization Head.

Due to the linking between semantic roles and syntactic roles (Dowty, 1991), the relations above overlap with syntactic roles, for example, Proto-Agent with Subject and Proto-Patient with Object, but they are not the same, as illustrated by the example 动物分类(*Animal Categorization*). Although the predicate 分类(*categorize*) in Chinese is an intransitive verb, the semantic relation between 动物(*animal*) and 分类(*categorization*) is Proto-Patient.

4 Paraphrase Patterns

4.1 Motivations

Syntactic patterns provide clues for semantic relations (Hearst, 1992). For example, Hearst(1992) uses the pattern "NP such as List" to indicate that nouns in List are hyponyms of NP. To classify the four semantic relations listed in section 3, we propose some domain independent surface paraphrase patterns to characterize each semantic relation. The patterns we adopted mainly exploit a set of word instances of prepositions, support verbs, feature nouns and aspect markers.

Prepositions are strong indicators of semantic roles in Chinese. For example, in sentence 1), the preposition 把(*ba*) indicates that the noun 门(*door*) and 张三(*Zhangsan*) is the Proto-Patient and Proto-Agent of verb 锁(*lock*) respectively.

1) a. 张三把门锁上
   b. *Zhangsan ba door locked.*
   c. *Zhangsan locked the door.*

The prepositions we use to characterize each relation are listed in table 2.

Relations	Prepositional Indicators
PP	被(bei), 让(rang), 叫(jiao), 由(you)
PA	把(ba), 将(jiang), 所(suo), 对(dui)
MA	通过(tongguo), 用(yong), 以(yi)
RA	在(zai), 于(yu), 从(cong)

Table 2: Prepositional indicators of different relations in Chinese.

Support verbs such as 进行(*conduct*), 加以(*put-to*) can take verb nominalizations as objects. When combined with prepositions, they could be good indicators of semantic roles. For example in 2), the verb 进行(*conduct*) together with the preposition 对(*dui*) indicate that the relation between 分类(*categorization*) and 动物(*animal*) is PA.

2) a. 对动物进行分类
   b. *dui animal conduct categorization.*
   c. *conduct categorization regarding animal.*

Nouns such as 方法(*method*), 方式(*manner*), 范围(*range*) and 地点(*place*) can be used as features when co-occurring with the compound nominalizations under consideration. For example, if 全球范围(*global range*) co-occurs frequently with 定位(*positioning*), it will indicate a possible RA relation between 全球(*global*) and 定位(*positioning*).

Another set of word instances we use is aspect, tense and modal markers. As we have mentioned, verb nominalizations have the same form as the corresponding verb predicates in Chinese. Aspect，tense and modal markers make a good indicator for recognizing a verb predicate. For example if a verb is directly followed by an aspect marker such as 了(*le*), which indicates a finished state, it could be safely viewed as a predicate. Such markers are very useful in paraphrase patterns. This can be illustrated by 3), in which, the tense marker 开始(*start*) indicates a strong agentive meaning of the noun 鸟类(*bird*) and provides good clues of the relation PP between鸟类(*bird*) and 迁徙(*migration*) in the compound 鸟类迁徙(*bird migration*).

3) a. 鸟类开始迁徙
   b. *Bird start migrate.*
   c. *Birds start to migrate.*

4.2 Paraphrase Pattern Templates

We use the set of word instances above to form pattern templates which could be instantiated by the compound nominalization under consideration to form paraphrase patterns. The templates are expressed using the employed search engine's query language. Currently, we employ totally 30 feature templates for the four semantic relations. A sample of the pattern templates is listed in Tabel 3, in which, x, y is the variable which need to be instantiated by the noun modifier and verb nominalization respectively.

Relations	Paraphrase Pattern Templates
PP	"对x进行y" ("*dui* x *conduct* y")
	"把x" "y" ("*ba* x" "y")
	"y着x" ("y *zhe* x")
	"x被" "y" ("x *bei*" "y")
PA	"被x" "y" ("*bei* x" "y")
	"x开始y" ("x *start* y")
	"x" "可以y" ("x" "*can* y")
	"x所y" ("x *suo* y")
MA	"通过x" "y" -"通过xy" ("*tongguo* x" "y" -"*tongguo* xy")
	"x方法" "y" ("x *method*" "y")
RA	"在x" "y" -"在y"("*zai* x" "y" -"*zai* y")
	"从x" "y" ("*cong* x" "y")
	"x范围" "y" ("x *range*" "y")

Table 3: A Sample Set of the Paraphrase Pattern Templates.

5 System Description

5.1 Data Source

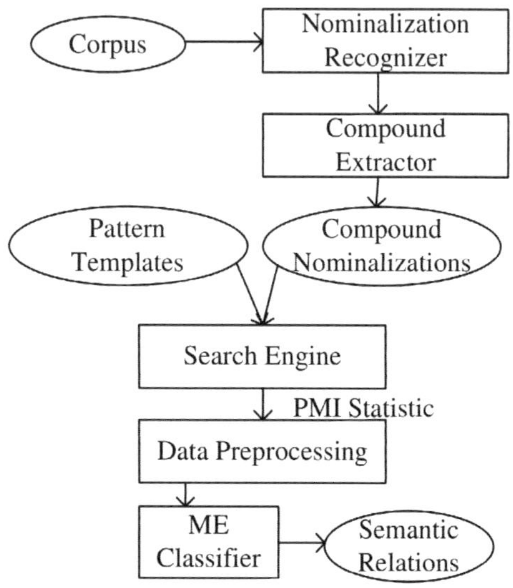

Figure 2: System Architecture

Figure 2 illustrates the system architecture of our approach. We view the semantic labeling of compound nominalization as a data-driven classification problem. The data used for the experiment is auto-extracted from the Chinese National Corpus (Jin et al., 2003), which is a balanced segmented and POS tagged corpus with 8M characters. Because the corpus doesn't distinguish verb predicates with verb nominalizations, a verb nominalization recognizer is first used to recognize all the verb nominalizations in the corpus, and then, a compound extractor identifies all the compound nominalizations having a noun modifier and a verb nominalization head in the corpus. We manually examined a sample of the result set and finally randomly select 300 correct noun-nominalization pairs as our training and testing set for semantic interpretation.

One PHD student majored in computer science and one in linguistics were employed to label all the 300 data samples simultaneously according to the relation set given in section 3. The annotator's agreement was measured using the Kappa statistic (Siegel and Castellan, 1988) illustrated in (1), of which $Pr(A)$ is the probability of the actual outcome and $Pr(E)$ is the probability of the expected outcome as predicted by chance. The Kappa score of the annotation is 87.3%.

$$K = \frac{Pr(A) - Pr(E)}{1 - Pr(E)} \quad (1)$$

After discussion, the two annotators reached agreement on a final version of the data sample labeling. In which, the proportion of relations PP, PA, MA, RA is 45.6%, 27.7%, 16.7% and 10% respectively, giving a baseline of 45.6% of the classification problem by viewing all the relations to be PP. Finally, the 300 data instances were partitioned into a training set and a testing set containing 225 and 75 instances respectively.

5.2 Maximum Entropy Model

We use the Maximum Entropy (ME) Model (Berger et al., 1996) for our classification task. Given a set of training examples of a random process, ME is a method of estimating the conditional probability $p(y|x)$ that, given a context x, the process will output y. In our task, the output corresponds to the four relation labels PP, PA, MA and RA.

The modeling of ME is based on the Maximum Entropy Principle, that is, modeling all that is known and assuming nothing about what is unknown. The computation of $p(y|x)$ is illustrated as the formula (2). $f_i(x, y)$ are binary valued feature functions with the parameter λ_i used to express the statistics of the data sample. $Z_\lambda(x)$ is a normalization factor.

$$p_\lambda(y|x) = \frac{1}{Z_\lambda(x)} \exp\left(\sum_i \lambda_i f_i(x, y)\right) \quad (2)$$

5.3 PMI-IR Score as Features

The feature functions we adopted for ME differentiate from most other works on the semantic labeling task, which mainly exploited features from well-parsed text. Instead, we use a web-based statistic called PMI-IR which mainly measures the co-occurrence between the data to classify and the set of paraphrase pattern templates we stated in section 4. The PMI-IR measure was first adopted by (Turney, 2001) for mining synonyms from the Web. (Etzioni et al., 2004) uses the PMI-IR measure to evaluate the information extracted from the Web.

Given a compound nominalization pair $p(x, y)$ and a set of paraphrase pattern templates t_1, t_2, ..., t_n, the PMI-IR score between p and t_i can be computed by formula (3).

$$PMI(p, t_i) = \frac{Hits(p, t_i)}{Hits(p)} \quad (3)$$

In which, $PMI(p, t_i)$ is the co-occurrence web page counts of $p(x, y)$ and t_i. For example, if the template t is "对(*dui*) x 进行(*conduct*) y" and the compound nominalization is the pair p(动物(*animal*),分类(*categorization*)), then $Hits(p, t)$ is the web counts returned from the search engine for the pattern "对(*dui*) 动物(*animal*) 进行(*conduct*) 分类(*categorization*)".

5.4 Scaling of PMI Features

Web counts are inflated which need to be scaled to attain a good estimation of the underlying probability density function in ME. In our approach, first, a log sub-linear transformation is used to preprocess the raw PMI-IR feature function for the ME model. Then, a discretization algorithm called CAIM (Kurgan and Cios, 2004) is used to transform the continuous feature functions into discrete ones.

CAIM is a supervised discretization algorithm which can discretize an attribute into the smallest number of intervals and maximize the class-attribute interdependency. Suppose that the data set consists of M examples and each example belongs to only one of the S classes. F indicates the continuous feature functions produced from paraphrase patterns in our task. D is a discretization scheme on F, which discretizes F into n non-overlapping discrete intervals. The class variable and the discretization variable of attribute F are treated as two random varibles defining a two-dimensional frequency matrix(called quanta matrix) that is shown in Table 4, in which, q_{ir} is the total number of continuous values belonging to the ith class that are within interval $(d_{r-1}, d_r]$, while M_{i+} is the total number of values belonging to the ith class, and M_{+r} is the total number of values of attribute F that are within the interval $(d_{r-1}, d_r]$, for $i = 1, 2, ..., S$ and $r = 1, 2, ..., n$. The CAIM algorithm uses a greedy search to find the specific discretization sechme D according to the Class-Attribute Interdependency Maximization (CAIM) criterion defined as(4), where max_r is the maximum value among all q_{ir} values.

Class	$[d_0,d_1]$	...	$[d_{r-1},d_r]$	...	$[d_{n-1},d_n]$	Class Total
C_1	q_{11}	...	q_{1r}	...	q_{1n}	M_{1+}
:	:	...	:	...	:	:
C_i	q_{i1}	...	q_{ir}	...	q_{in}	M_{i+}
:	:	...	:	...	:	:
C_s	q_{S1}	...	q_{Sr}	...	q_{Sn}	M_{S+}
Interval Total	M_{+1}	...	M_{+r}	...	M_{+n}	M

Table 4: The Quanta Matrix for Attribute F and Discretization Scheme D

$$CAIM(C,D|F) = \frac{1}{n}\sum_{r=1}^{n}\frac{\max_r^2}{M_{+r}} \quad (4)$$

6 Results and Discussion

In this section, we present our experimental results on the semantic relation labeling of our Compound Nominalization Dataset. We compared the performance between two different engines, also, between the raw PMI and the scaled one.

Two search engines, Google (www.google.com) and Baidu (www.baidu.com) are used and compared to obtain the PMI scores between a verb nominalization pair and the set of paraphrase patterns. The result of using Google and Baidu are comparable. For example, when using raw PMI score as the features of ME classification model, Google based algorithm obtains a correct classification rate of 65.3%, while Baidu based algorithm obtains a correct classification rate of 62.7%. The main difference between the two search engines is their indexing and rating algorithm of the web pages. Compared to Google, Baidu uses a stop wordlist, including empty markers such as 了 (*le*), to filter the queries. While this is beneficial for common users, it hurts our algorithm which depends heavily on such information.

Compared with using raw PMI as the classification features, feature scaling improves much on the classification result. Using Log transformation, Both Google based and Baidu based algorithm increase about 4 percent on the correct classification rate and when CAIM algorithm is employed to preprocess the data, both algorithm's correct classification rates increase more than 8 percent. We think that the usefulness of log sub-linear transformation is mainly due to the fact that the Web is extremely biased and inflated. The compression of the inflated feature space can enable the ME model to give a good estimation of the underlying probability density function of the data. As to the usefulness of the discretization of the data, we think that it is mainly because that the web-based statistics contain much noise and the features produced from paraphrase patterns are highly correlated with specific classes. CAIM discretization algorithm can maximize the class-attribute interdependence in the data and can be seen as a noise pruning process in some sense.

Among the four semantic relations labeled, PP gets the best precision and recall overall and relations such as RA gets a lower F-score. We think that this is mainly due to the difficulty in selecting paraphrase patterns for RA compared to PP. Some patterns are not as indicative as others for the relations considered. For example, the paraphrase patterns "在x" "y" -"在y" ("in x" "y" -"in y") for RA is not as indicative as the pattern "对x进行y" (*dui x conduct y*) for PP. Discovering and selecting the most indicative patterns for each relation is the key element for our algorithm.

We can make a rough comparison to the related works in the literature. In syntactic relation labeling of compound nominalization in English, Lapata (2000) and Grover et al. (2005) both apply parsed text and obtains 87.3%, 77% accuracy for the subject-object and subject-object-prepositional objects classification tasks respectively. Nicholson (2005) uses both the parsed text and the web for the classification of subject-object-prepositional objects and the result is comparatively poor. Compared to such works, the relations we exploited in the labeling task is purely semantic which makes the classification task more difficult and we don't use any parsed text as input. Considering the difficulty of

	Google			Baidu		
	Precision	Recall	F-Score	precision	Recall	F-Score
			Raw PMI			
PP	72.5	82.9	77.3	65.3	88.9	75.2
PA	47.6	50.0	48.8	50.0	42.1	45.7
MA	75.0	50.0	60.0	50.0	27.3	35.3
RA	66.7	50.0	57.1	80.0	44.4	57.1
Rate	65.3			62.7		
			Log			
PP	66.7	85.7	75.0	68.2	83.3	75.0
PA	64.7	55.0	59.5	60.0	47.4	52.9
MA	80.0	66.7	72.7	66.7	54.5	60.0
RA	100	37.5	54.5	71.4	55.5	62.5
Rate	69.3			66.7		
			Log+Discretization			
PP	82.5	94.3	88.0	80.9	94.4	87.2
PA	81.3	65.0	72.2	64.7	57.9	61.1
MA	75.0	50.0	60.0	87.5	63.6	73.7
RA	54.5	75.0	63.2	64.5	55.6	58.8
Rate	77.3			76.0		

Table 5: Results comparing different search engines, raw PMI as features vs. scaled features. Rate is the correct classification rate for the four semantic relations overall.

the problem and the unsupervised nature of our algorithm, the results (accuracy 77.3%) are very encouraging.

7 Conclusions and Future Work

In this paper, we view the semantic relation labeling of compound nominalization as a classification problem. We propose four coarse-grained semantic roles of the noun modifier for the verb nominalization head. A Maximum Entropy model is applied for the classification task. The features used for the model are web-based statistics acquired via class related paraphrase patterns, which mainly use a set of word instances of prepositions, support verbs, feature nouns and aspect markers. The experimental result illustrates that our method is very effective.

We believe that the method we proposed is not only limited in the semantic interpretation of compound nominalizations, but can also be used as a way to compensate the low accuracy of the more general task of semantic role labeling of nominalization phrases caused by the inefficiency of Chinese parsers.

The major limitation of our approach is that the paraphrase pattern templates we use now are hand-coded according to the linguistic theory. To achieve more generality of our method, in the future, we should study automatic template induction and feature selection algorithms for the classifier to select the set of most indicative pattern templates for each semantic relation.

8 Acknowledgements

This work is supported by NSFC Major Research Program 60496326: Basic Theory and Core Techniques of Non Canonical Knowledge.

References

A.L. Berger, V.J. Della Pietra, and S.A. Della Pietra. 1996. A maximum entropy approach to natural language processing. *Computational Linguistics*, 22(1):39–71.

D.A. Dahl, M.S. Palmer, and R.J. Passonneau. 1987. Nominalizations in PUNDIT. *Proceedings of the 25th Annual Meeting of the Association for Computational Linguistics, Stanford University, Stanford, CA, July*.

DR Dowty. 1991. Thematic ProtoRoles and Argument Selection. *Second Conference on Maritime Termonology, Turku*, 33:31–38.

O. Etzioni, M. Cafarella, D. Downey, S. Kok, A.M. Popescu, T. Shaked, S. Soderland, D.S. Weld, and A. Yates. 2004. Web-scale information extraction in knowitall:(preliminary results). *Proceedings of the 13th international conference on World Wide Web*, pages 100–110.

T.W. Finin. 1980. The semantic interpretation of compound nominals. *Dissertation Abstracts International Part B: Science and Engineering[DISS. ABST. INT. PT. B- SCI. & ENG.]*,, 41(6):1980.

G. Grefenstette and J. Nioche. 2000. Estimation of English and non-English Language Use on the WWW. *Arxiv preprint cs.CL/0006032*.

C. Grover, A. Lascarides, and M. Lapata. 2005. A comparison of parsing technologies for the biomedical domain. *Natural Language Engineering*, 11(01):27–65.

M.A. Hearst. 1992. Automatic acquisition of hyponyms from large text corpora. *Proceedings of the 14th conference on Computational linguistics-Volume 2*, pages 539–545.

R.D. Hull and F. Gomez. 1996. Semantic interpretation of nominalizations. *AAAI Conference*, pages 1062–1068.

Guangjin Jin, Shulun Guo, Hang Xiao, and Yunfan Zhang. 2003. Standardization for Corpus Processing. *Applied Linguistics*, pages 16–24.

R. Jones and R. Ghani. 2000. Automatically building a corpus for a minority language from the web. *Proceedings of the Student Research Workshop at the 38th Annual Meeting of the Association for Computational Linguistics*, pages 29–36.

F. Keller and M. Lapata. 2003. Using the web to obtain frequencies for unseen bigrams. *Computational Linguistics*, 29(3):459–484.

S.N. Kim and T. Baldwin. 2005. Automatic interpretation of noun compounds using WordNet similarity. *Proc. of IJCNLP-05*, pages 945–956.

S.N. Kim and T. Baldwin. 2006. Interpreting Semantic Relations in Noun Compounds via Verb Semantics. *Proceedings of the COLING/ACL 2006 Main Conference Poster Sessions*, pages 491–498.

LA Kurgan and KJ Cios. 2004. CAIM discretization algorithm. *Knowledge and Data Engineering, IEEE Transactions on*, 16(2):145–153.

M. Lapata. 2000. The automatic interpretation of nominalizations. *Proceedings of AAAI*.

M. Lauer. 1995. *Designing Statistical Language Learners: Experiments on Compound Nouns*. Ph.D. thesis, Ph. D. thesis, Macquarie University, Sydney.

R. Leonard. 1984. *The interpretation of English noun sequences on the computer*. North-Holland.

D.B. Mcdonald. 1982. Understanding noun compounds. *Carnegie-Mellon University*.

D. Moldovan, A. Badulescu, M. Tatu, D. Antohe, and R. Girju. 2004. Models for the semantic classification of noun phrases. *Proceedings of HLT/NAACL-2004 Workshop on Computational Lexical Semantics*.

J. Nicholson. 2005. *Statistical Interpretation of Compound Nouns*. Ph.D. thesis, University of Melbourne.

S. Pradhan, H. Sun, W. Ward, J.H. Martin, and D. Jurafsky. 2004. Parsing Arguments of Nominalizations in English and Chinese. *Proc. of HLT-NAACL*.

B. Rosario and M. Hearst. 2001. Classifying the semantic relations in noun compounds via a domain-specific lexical hierarchy. *Proceedings of the 2001 Conference on Empirical Methods in Natural Language Processing (EMNLP-01)*, pages 82–90.

S. Siegel and NJ Castellan. 1988. Nonparametric statistics for the behavioral sciences. *McGraw-HiU Book Company, New York*.

JF Sowa. 1984. *Conceptual structures: information processing in mind and machine*. Addison-Wesley Longman Publishing Co., Inc. Boston, MA, USA.

P.D. Turney. 2001. Mining the Web for synonyms: PMI-IR versus LSA on TOEFL. *Proceedings of the Twelfth European Conference on Machine Learning*, pages 491–502.

P.D. Turney. 2005. Measuring semantic similarity by latent relational analysis. *Proceedings of the Nineteenth International Joint Conference on Artificial Intelligence (IJCAI-05)*, pages 1136–1141.

L.H. Vanderwende. 1995. *The analysis of noun sequences using semantic information extracted from online dictionaries*. Ph.D. thesis, Georgetown University.

N. Xue. 2006. Semantic Role Labeling of Nominalized Predicates in Chinese. *Proceedings of the Human Language Technology Conference of the North American Chapter of the ACL*.

X. Zhu and R. Rosenfeld. 2001. Improving trigram language modeling with the World Wide Web. *Acoustics, Speech, and Signal Processing, 2001. Proceedings.(ICASSP'01). 2001 IEEE International Conference on*, 1.

Author Index